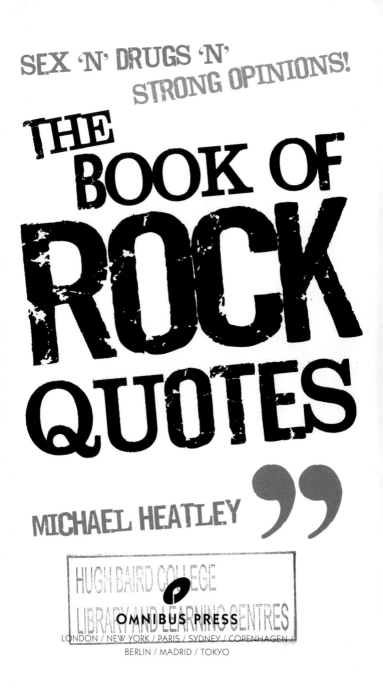

SEX 'N' DRUGS 'N'
STRONG OPINIONS!

# THE
# BOOK OF
# ROCK
# QUOTES

MICHAEL HEATLEY **"**

**OMNIBUS PRESS**

LONDON / NEW YORK / PARIS / SYDNEY / COPENHAGEN /
BERLIN / MADRID / TOKYO

Copyright © 2008 Omnibus Press
(A Division of Music Sales Limited)

Cover designed by Fresh Lemon
Picture research by Sarah Bacon
All images by LFI

ISBN: 978.1.84772.418.2
Order No: OP 52448

**Exclusive Distributors**
Music Sales Limited,
14/15 Berners Street,
London, W1T 3LJ.

**Music Sales Corporation,**
257 Park Avenue South,
New York, NY 10010, USA.

**Macmillan Distribution Services,**
53 Park West Drive,
Derrimut, Vic 3030,
Australia.

Every effort has been made to trace the copyright
holders of the photographs in this book but one or two
were unreachable. We would be grateful if the
photographers concerned would contact us.

Printed by Gutenberg Press Ltd, Malta

A catalogue record for this book is available from the
British Library.

Visit Omnibus Press on the web at
www.omnibuspress.com

# CONTENTS

"DOWNLOADING? I'VE NEVER DONE IT. IMAGINE ZEPPELIN WITHOUT THE ALBUM COVERS. TERRIBLE."

JIMMY PAGE, LED ZEPPELIN

# CHAPTER ONE
# THE ROCK
# DON'T STOP...

**"** I'm a rocker — I don't want to work. I want to goof off. **"**
CHRISSIE HYNDE, THE PRETENDERS

**"** I hate most of what constitutes rock music, which is basically middle-aged crap. **"** STING

**"** Does it mean this, does it mean that, that's all anybody wants to know. Fuck them, darling. I say what any decent poet would say if you dared ask him to analyse his work: If you see it, dear, then it's there. **"** FREDDIE MERCURY, QUEEN

**"** I have never tried to write this thing called a song that's played on radios all around the world, that window-cleaners hum, that people listen to in traffic jams. I was never interested in song: U2 came about through a sound. **"** BONO, U2

**"** I've always said that pop music is disposable and it is, and that's the fun of pop music. If it wasn't disposable, it'd be a pain in the fuckin' arse. **"** ELTON JOHN

**"** I don't ever want to do anything mediocre. Learning from music is like eating a meal – you have to pace yourself. You can't take everything from it all at once. I want to be different, definitely. I'm not a one trick pony. I'm at least a five-trick pony. **"** AMY WINEHOUSE

**Forget about the tired old myth that rock'n'roll is just making records, pulling birds, getting pissed and having a good time. That's not what it's all about.**

PETE TOWNSHEND, THE WHO

The music is all. People should die for it. People are dying for everything else, so why not the music? **LOU REED**

**I'd be too embarrassed to write something like 'We're all going down the pub', even though it is probably very real for thousands of kids. I just feel I should reach for something higher. I think music is an art form. A highly abused art form.** PAUL WELLER, THE JAM

I've always found it weird that people take it so seriously. I don't think rock music is silly, but I think it should be treated with the irreverence it deserves. **BOB GELDOF**

JOHNNY CASH

**There's a lot of things blamed on me that never happened. But then there's a lot of things that I did that I never got caught at.**

JOHNNY CASH

Punk Rock? Oh, I've been in it for years, dear... Actually I saw the Sex Pistols at the 100 Club and I thought they were pretty good. Well, not good, but y'know, they could be. **MICK JAGGER**

**❝** I hate art. I can't stand it. It's treating something that's supposed to be good as precious. And it ain't precious. Anyone can make a record. **❞** JOHN LYDON

**❝** It only takes an hour to write a song. You can play everything inside of three weeks. Everyone knows it's dead easy. **❞** JOE STRUMMER, THE CLASH

**❝** Bono told me, 'Spare us the "interesting" second album'. So our plan is simple – make every song bigger and better than **Hot Fuss.❞** BRANDON FLOWERS, THE KILLERS

**❝** Rock'n'roll is not just music. You're selling an attitude, too. Take away the attitude and you're just like anyone else. The kids need a sense of adventure and rock'n'roll gives it to them. **❞ MALCOLM McLAREN, MANAGER, SEX PISTOLS**

# "MUSIC IS... WELL, I KNOW IT'S BETTER THAN WORKING IN FORD'S." IAN DURY

**❝** I don't understand why people think it's so incredibly difficult to learn to play a guitar. I found it incredibly easy. You just pick a chord, go twang and you've got music. **❞**
**SID VICIOUS**

**❝** I love rock'n'roll. I think it's an exciting art form. It's revolutionary. Still revolutionary and it changed people. It changed their hearts. But yeah, even rock'n'roll has a lot of rubbish, really bad music. **❞**
NICK CAVE, NICK CAVE & THE BAD SEEDS

**❝** It ain't punk, it ain't New Wave. It's the next step and the logical progression for groups to move in. Call it what you want – all the terms stink. Just call it rock'n'roll. **❞**
**MICK JONES, THE CLASH**

**If you can't say it in a three-minute song, you can't say it at all.** NODDY HOLDER, SLADE

If you can really get it together in three minutes... that's what pop songs are all about. **DEBBIE HARRY, BLONDIE**

**I don't think anybody steals anything; all of us borrow.**
BB KING

Without freedom of expression, good taste means nothing. **NEIL YOUNG**

**The world doesn't need another posturing clown yammering away about his 'baby'.**
DAVID BYRNE, TALKING HEADS

The definition of rock'n'roll lies here for me: if it screams for truth rather than help, if it commits itself with a courage that it can't be sure it really has, if it stands up and admits something is wrong but doesn't insist on blood, then it is rock'n'roll. **PETE TOWNSHEND, THE WHO**

## "MUSIC IS A SAFE KIND OF HIGH."
JIMI HENDRIX

I never really did anything that outrageous on stage. The hanging had been done ten million times in every Western. The guillotine had been done since 1925 in vaudeville shows. It's just the fact that it had rock'n'roll behind it that made it sound so damn notorious. **ALICE COOPER**

**Everyone just wants more and more information. All the fantasy's gone out of music, 'cos everything is too fucking real. Every album comes with a DVD with some cunt going, 'Yeah well, we tried the drums over there,**

but...' Give a shit, man! It makes people seem too human, whereas I was brought up on Marc Bolan and David Bowie, and it was like, 'Do they actually come from fucking Mars?' **"**

NOEL GALLAGHER, OASIS

JAKE SHEARS

**"** Rock'n'roll isn't even music, really. It's a mistreating of instruments to get feelings over. **"**

**MARK E SMITH, THE FALL**

**"** It's a bitch convincing people to like you. **"**

JAKE SHEARS, SCISSOR SISTERS

**"** Messages become a drag, like preaching. I think one of the worst possible beliefs is that pop stars know any more about life than anyone else. The thing to do is to move people, to really turn them on, to subject them to a fantastic experience, to stretch their imagination. **"**

**NICK MASON, PINK FLOYD**

**"** In the early days, DeeDee would shout '1-2-3-4' and all the band would start playing a different song. Then we'd throw the instruments around and walk off. And it wasn't put-on, either. But it became easy. It became drilled into us. What the hell, it's all the same song anyhow. **"**

TOMMY RAMONE

**"** That's the biggest problem with the last fifteen years of rock – people claim it's art, and it's not. **"** **ELVIS COSTELLO**

**❝I don't see that rock'n'roll should be a bad influence on anyone. It's just entertainment and the kids who like to identify their youthful high spirits with a solid beat are thus possible avoiding other pursuits which could be harmful to them.❞** BILL HALEY

❝I love music, but I don't pride myself on being a musician. I pride myself on entertainment and my presentation. I tried to master rock because it's the most appropriate form for me to do anything in. It suits me.❞

**MARILYN MANSON**

GENE SIMMONS

**❝The stage is a holy place, you do not get up there and degrade it.❞**

GENE SIMMONS, KISS

❝I hate to say this, but at the time, (late 1970s) it was like the smart people liked punk and the dumb people liked Journey.❞

**HOWIE KLEIN, PRESIDENT, REPRISE RECORDS**

**❝It can be explained in just one word – 'sincerity'. When a hillbilly sings a crazy song, he feels crazy. When he sings 'I Laid My Mother Away' he sees her a-laying right there in the coffin... you got to know a lot about hard work. You got to have smelt a lot of mule manure before you can sing like a hillbilly.❞**

HANK WILLIAMS

ALBUM COMES
BOUT YOUR SONGS AND YOU'RE NEVER GOING TO GET

"Music completely changed my life, punk rock made me so much more aware of things that I couldn't believe it. It finally reminded me that I've had an identity all along. It changed my fucking life when I heard it. So it's a totally important thing, it's just that people blow it out of all proportion." **KURT COBAIN, NIRVANA**

**"Rock music has to be naive. And when you're no longer musically naive, or socially naive, or intellectually naive, and you start to get a bit more worldly-wise, no way can you do that any more."** IAN ANDERSON, JETHRO TULL

"Rock'n'roll is about cocks and jiving and the old bloody nose... and about people like us talking seriously about the social order." **JEAN JACQUES BURNEL, THE STRANGLERS**

**"We're not perfectionist, we're idealists. We think that rock'n'roll is more than just music for the kids."** PETE TOWNSHEND, THE WHO,

## "DON'T INTERPRET ME. MY SONGS DON'T HAVE ANY MEANING. THEY'RE JUST WORDS." BOB DYLAN

**"My ambition is to have as many guitars as Rick Wakeman has sparkles on his cape. I saw him playing in the States. He was pushing a Mellotron over an ice rink on skates, trying to catch it. That's art."** RICK NEILSON, CHEAP TRICK

"I'm just not a tortured, frustrated person who has to pour all of these things out of his soul. None of that is a prerequisite to being good at rock'n'roll." **DAVE GILMOUR, PINK FLOYD**

**The movie Spinal Tap rocked my world. It's for rock what The Sound Of Music was for hills. They really nailed how dumb rock can be.** JACK BLACK, TENACIOUS D

I didn't write 'School Day' in a classroom. I wrote it in the Street Hotel, one of the big, black, low-priced hotels in St. Louis. **CHUCK BERRY**

**The music that is being played on the radio every day damages people. There's no doubt in my mind about that.** VAN MORRISON

I'll never get tired of playing this music. I'm never gonna stop playing it. I'll go on playing just as long as there are people to listen. **JERRY LEE LEWIS**

# "ROCK'N'ROLL IS INSTANT COFFEE."

BOB GELDOF

Rock hasn't progressed. Progression was Miles Davis playing modals and you can't do that in rock. Progression was Coltrane and you can't do that in rock. **CHARLIE WATTS, THE ROLLING STONES**

**Mild barbarians is how we were once described, and I can't really deny it.** JIMMY PAGE, LED ZEPPELIN

Rock'n'roll is the music that inspired me to play music. There is nothing conceptually better than rock'n'roll. No group, be it The Beatles, Dylan or the Stones have ever improved on 'Whole Lotta Shakin' for my money.

**JOHN LENNON**

**I like ballads and I know people that like them too. I'm hip to the fact that people like a love song.**

PAUL McCARTNEY

❝I don't see us being in that rock'n'roll tradition at all. In fact I don't like rock'n'roll. The attitude and leather jacket. It's old hat. It's redneck. Think about it, all the biggest rock groups in the world are rednecks, white Anglo-Saxons: Bon Jovi, Guns N'Roses, U2. The frightening thing is people all over the world relate to that rubbish.❞

**IAN BROWN, STONE ROSES**

❝**You know, the rock revolution did happen, it really did. Trouble was nobody realised.**❞ DAVID BOWIE

❝Most rock guitarists play twenty notes where one would do. I can't do that, unless I speeded up the tape. I just try to bluff my way through the fast bits and hope it comes off. None of us are virtuosos on our instruments. If we tried other styles we couldn't do it.❞ **DAVE GILMOUR, PINK FLOYD**

IAN BROWN

"SCHOOL IS PRACTICE FOR FUTURE LIFE, PRACTICE MAKES PERFECT AND NOBODY'S PERFECT, SO WHY PRACTICE?"

BILLIE JOE ARMSTRONG, GREEN DAY

# CHAPTER TWO
# THE KIDS ARE ALL RIGHT

**I was a veteran before I was a teenager.** MICHAEL JACKSON

My teenage years were exactly what they were supposed to be. Everybody has their own path. It's laid out for you. It's just up to you to walk it. JUSTIN TIMBERLAKE

**My old report cards were concerned with my hyperactivity. The teachers all said, 'David could be a very good student if he could just stay in one place and sit still.' There were lots of requests for my mom to come in and talk about it.** DAVE GROHL, NIRVANA

Public school gives you incredible hang-ups about encounters with the opposite sex. It just sets you up for conceiving the woman as only two things: the whore or the princess. I learned how to survive in public school.
PETER GABRIEL

**My parents wanted me to be a lawyer. But I don't think I would have been very happy. I'd be in front of the jury singing.** JENNIFER LOPEZ

My dad was very strict and taught me I must always respect my elders. I couldn't speak unless I was spoken to first by grown-ups. So I've always been very quiet.
JIMI HENDRIX

66 The thing about us is we're honest. If we're asked whether we take drugs, we say yes. I was brought up by my mam not to be a liar. 99 NOEL GALLAGHER, OASIS

66 I was expelled from school, but I was the teacher's pet in English because I was very good at it. We had this lady teacher. I don't think it was sexual. She put me in this storeroom with the GCSE English paper when I was 13 and I passed it by 20 per cent. 99 **LEMMY, MOTÖRHEAD**

66 I wanted to have a place that I could create everything that I never had as a child. So, you see rides. You see animals. There's a movie theatre. I was always on tour, travelling. 99 MICHAEL JACKSON

66 **IT'S LIKE GETTING A LOUIS VUITTON HANDBAG... SHE BOUGHT A BABY, FOR GOD'S SAKE.** 99

**SHARON OSBOURNE, ON MADONNA'S ADOPTION**

66 Sometimes life's so much cooler when you just don't know any better and all the painful lessons have not hammered your head open yet. 99

ANTHONY KIEDIS, RED HOT CHILI PEPPERS

66 So I get on this fucking train one morning and there's Jagger and under his arm he has four or five albums. I haven't seen him since the time I bought an ice-cream off him and we haven't hung around together since we were five, six, ten years old. We recognised each other straight off... and under his arm he's got Chuck Berry and Little Walter, Muddy Waters... 99

**KEITH RICHARDS ON MEETING MICK JAGGER**

ROBERT SMITH

**❝ I decided at seven that all my surroundings sucked, that there was no sign of anybody who would be into art or music. ❞**

KURT COBAIN, NIRVANA

**❝ I became an adult in an extreme way. I was recently sorting some old photographs and I found another Robert Smith wearing make-up, charicatural and aggressive. I didn't invent this character: he escaped from me. My anger is still the same, but I make it positive. ❞** ROBERT SMITH, THE CURE

**❝ John played all this stuff and I remember thinking he smelled a bit drunk. Quite a nice chap, but he was still a bit drunk. ❞** PAUL McCARTNEY

**❝ Being in the Spice Girls is like having four older sisters. They all look after me and I couldn't dream of leaving them. ❞** EMMA BUNTON, SPICE GIRLS

**❝ I started Michael (Jackson) years ago. I saw him in Gary, Indiana, and we'd have him on the talent shows. He kind of emulated me, and did the best he could. ❞** JAMES BROWN

**❝ Because of the artificial popularity that they (the music press) have created out of punk rock, they have broken the backs of young people for the next two or three years who really have got some genuine artistry to offer. They will have the label 'punk' stuck on them, no matter what they do. ❞** IAN ANDERSON, JETHRO TULL

**In the early years, I found a voice that was my voice and also partly my father's voice. But isn't that what you always do? Why do kids at five years old go into the closet and put their daddy's shoes on? Hey, my kids do it. They run in the car and come out clunking along with your boots on. And I think that was part of what I was doing. Then you go beyond it and find your own life.**
BRUCE SPRINGSTEEN

I never was a teenager. I don't remember doing any teenage songs. **MICK JAGGER**

**I don't know what it is – I just fell into it really. My daddy and I were laughing about it the other day. He looked at me and said 'The last thing I can remember is I was working in a can factory and you were driving a truck.'**
ELVIS PRESLEY

I am the product of a haphazard musical environment which, I suppose, makes me a folk artist. **JAMES TAYLOR**

**When I was a kid, really small, I saw my brother go to the bathroom. I'll never forget it. I tried to do it too... I stood over the toilet and tried to 'do it' the same way. My mother came in and tried to explain. I was outraged and demanded to know if he did it, why couldn't I? I'm twenty three, and I still haven't changed. I want to know why I can't do it all.** SUZI QUATRO

I was very vicious, aggressive. I was a bastard, I was a real cunt. I really was. I mean, it was the law of the jungle where I came from. That's how it used to be and that's how I was. **ROGER DALTREY, THE WHO**

**The thing is, if my father hadn't been strict I wouldn't be who I am today. I think... I think that his strictness**

**taught me a certain amount of discipline that has helped me in my life and my career and also made me work harder for things, whether for acceptance or the privilege to do things.**  MADONNA

He changes so, doesn't he? He's changing his views about everything all the time. He's like a chameleon. There'll never be a dictatorship here and why he says he wants one, I don't know.  **MRS JONES ON HER SON, DAVID BOWIE**

**My dad was a really straight dude but he was a jazz freak. I was always surrounded by culture and music and literature so I was definitely the exception in my neighbourhood. I didn't grow up a complete idiot.**
DAVE GROHL, NIRVANA

The copper came to the door to tell us about the accident. It was just like it's supposed to be, the way it is in the films. Asking if I were her son and all that. Then he told us and we both went white. It was the worst thing that ever happened to me.
**JOHN LENNON, ON HIS MOTHER'S DEATH IN A ROAD ACCIDENT IN 1958**

## I LEFT SCHOOL AT 17 AND WAS A STAR BY THE TIME I WAS 18 – IN CERTAIN PARTS OF THE WORLD ANYWAY.

GEORGE MICHAEL

Where I came from, anyone with the least bit extrovert tendencies became a footballer, a boxer, a rock musician or a thief. If I hadn't found rock'n'roll, I'd have ended up a criminal, 'cos I'm not very good at football.
**ROGER DALTREY, THE WHO**

**" I first realised I could sing at two years of age. I was eight years old and they entered me in a talent competition. I wore glasses, no music and I won. I got a whipping the same day, my mother whipped me for something. Destroyed my ego completely. "** ELVIS PRESLEY

**"** I've had the responsibility since I was 15 of someone who is 25 or 30, so now I have a lot of pressure. I employ a lot of people, I make a lot of adult decisions, and that has forced me to grow up a little faster. **"** BEYONCE

**" I only met my son recently... Before that, I wasn't good enough. He didn't need a junkie, a pill addict, or a slobbering quaalude idiot hanging around him. "** IGGY POP

**"** He was the vilest geezer I ever met – all misshapen, no hair, hunchback, flat feet. Everybody hated him. Everybody hated me. We hated each other, too, but nobody else would talk to us so we'd just get drunk and criticise each other. **"** SID VICIOUS, ON JOHNNY ROTTEN

**" It's all right as long as he doesn't smoke or drink alcohol. I know all about his girlfriends. "**
MRS SIMMONS, MOTHER OF KISS'S GENE SIMMONS

**"** I didn't come from a trailer park. I grew up middle class and my dad had money and my mom made my lunch. I got a car when I was sixteen. I'm proud of that. **"** KID ROCK

**" I had a plastic Beatle wig when I was very small. That's what started me buying records. "** JOHNNY ROTTEN

**"** I threw a real fit at a recent awards show. They gave my band just meat and cheese to eat and wouldn't allow us time to rehearse for our spot. Now, if you've been to upper-class schools or you're an actress like Gwyneth

Paltrow, you get treated well. But us rock kids are considered to be uneducated, so the attitude is to treat us like crap. **" COURTNEY LOVE**

**" When I was two feet off the ground, I collected broken glass and cats. When I was three feet off the ground, I made drawings of animals and forest fires. When I was four feet off the ground I discovered boys and bicycles. "** JONI MITCHELL

**"** When I was a kid, my mother and father never told me they loved me or that they were proud of me, so all I'm doing is what I would have liked. I've said to Jack I'm not your father, I'm the best friend you've got in the world, because I love you more than life itself. **"** OZZY OSBOURNE

**" For most people, the fantasy is driving around in a big car, having all the chicks you want and being able to pay for it. It always has been, still is, and always will be. And anyone who says it isn't is talking bullshit. "** MICK JAGGER

**"** I like punk... things have changed, but the things that made me angry as a kid make me angry now. **"** ROGER DALTREY, THE WHO

**" All through my early years, my father kept telling me he would hire a prostitute for me to lose my virginity to on my sixteenth birthday. I was really scared at that prospect because I was scared of prostitutes, and so I tried my hardest to lose my virginity before I reached 16. I managed it just before I turned 16, and when I told my father I think he was a little disappointed. "** MARILYN MANSON

**"** Michael could be a very good impersonator if he wanted to; he could probably make a living from it. **"** MRS EVA JAGGER

**"My past is so complicated you wouldn't believe it."**

BOB DYLAN

# "MY BASIC OUTLOOK IS STILL MUCH THE SAME AS IT WAS WHEN I WAS FOURTEEN." DAVID BOWIE

**"My first memory is being about five, at school, and being asked to give out the school milk. And I refused to do it. I said, 'No – just put the milk crate on the desk. Everybody can get their own.' ... In the end, that's what they did – I changed the system!"** IAN BROWN, STONE ROSES

**"**I think I had one voice lesson. The teacher told me not to take any more because it might affect my delivery.**"**

**JOHNNY CASH**

**"Hibbing's a good ol' town, I ran away from it when I was ten, twelve, thirteen, fifteen, fifteen and a half, seventeen and eighteen. I been caught an' brought back all but once."** BOB DYLAN

**"**Many people ask what are The Beatles? Why the Beatles? Ugh, Beatles? How did the name arrive? So we will tell you. It came in a vision: a man appeared on a flaming pie and said unto them 'from now on you are Beatles with an A'. 'Thank you, Mister Man', they said, thanking him. And so they were Beatles.**"** **JOHN LENNON**

**"I was a bit of a rogue when I was young. I used to wag school and be into fuckin' glue-sniffing and stuff. Then me and this lad robbed our corner shop, which is a very stupid thing to do 'cos everyone knows exactly who you are. Anyway, I was put on probation and I got grounded for six months."** NOEL GALLAGHER, OASIS

" After reading Tolkien, I just had to have a place in the country. " **ROBERT PLANT, LED ZEPPELIN**

**" At that time, Cassius Clay, as he was known, was the greatest thing. If you were black, all you had to do was jump in a ring, shuffle around a bit, and everybody would be scared of you. But, looking around, I could see that the tough guy with the thick ear wasn't getting the chicks, while your man up on the stage seemed to be doing OK. "** PHIL LYNOTT, THIN LIZZY

" I used to see them drivers with their shirts off, handkerchiefs around their neck, a little cap on their head. They looked daring to me. I always dreamed of being a real wild truck driver. " **ELVIS PRESLEY**

**" Me and me dad were going to a football match and me dad came out in this old coat, and it was rough. It was an old black coat and he had outgrown it and me mum said, 'You can't go out in that bloody old coat! Your son's a millionaire, you'll disgrace the street'. "** ROD STEWART

" I like my name, but I want to change it to Susie, though. " **CHINA SLICK, DAUGHTER OF GRACE, ORIGINALLY NAMED 'GOD'**

**" I love Michael Jackson. The quality of his voice is fantastic. He's the only kid I really like in that respect. Michael Jackson had it when he was one. "** RINGO STARR

RINGO STARR

" I didn't even know the 'Summer of Love' was happening. I was too busy playing with my Action Man. " **SID VICIOUS**

"YOU CAN ONLY LIVE
ONE DREAM AT A TIME."

DIANA ROSS

# CHAPTER THREE
# CASH...
# OR CREDIBILITY?

" I won't speak to the teen mags because all they want to talk about is hairspray and stuff, and it's all just a crock of shit. I don't want to sell the band on that. " JON BON JOVI

" Street credibility is full of shit. It's something journalists invented to pass the time of day. Anyone who claims to have street credibility is lying through his teeth. "
**STEWART COPELAND, THE POLICE**

" The colleges have to be destroyed, they're dangerous. Doctors trying to cure the freaks while they gulp pills. Rushing with the music. It's the music that kept us all intact... kept us from going crazy. You should have two radios – in case one gets broken. " LOU REED

" My life is the street where I walk. " **BOB DYLAN**

" The people of America are just not born with culture. "
PHIL SPECTOR

" You can't be a feminist and live in a mansion. "
**BONNIE RAITT**

" If any of our songs ever did make it on the Top 10, I'd disband the group immediately. " ROBERT SMITH, THE CURE

ALEX TURNER

“We didn't play **Top Of The Pops** because we just didn't feel like it at the time. Again, it just didn't seem like our thing. It's a bit shit. We'd have felt a bit silly doing it. We didn't need to squeeze the extra sales out - so it was like, 'Why do it?' I don't know if we'll ever do it - I doubt we will now, because it's got blown out of proportion. If we ever did it, it would be like 'Arctic Monkeys Sell Out!'”

**ALEX TURNER, ARCTIC MONKEYS**

“**There are a lot of things you have to sacrifice. It all depends on how deep you want to get into whatever your gig is.**” JIMI HENDRIX

“It was just like being in The Monkees.”

**GLEN MATLOCK, FORMER SEX PISTOL**

“**I want records out. I want hit records but I won't eat shit. There's certain things you have to do, but I won't eat shit. I've been shat on while I'm not looking, but I've never eaten shit.**” MICK JONES, THE CLASH

“People will offer us crazy things, like, go play some birthday party in Barcelona and they'll give us a half-million dollars. We're always doing shit like that.”

**WAYNE COYNE, THE FLAMING LIPS**

“**A cult figure is a guy who hasn't got the musical ability to make it into the charts.**” JOHN CALE

**❝**Colleges are like old age homes, except for the fact that more people die in colleges.**❞** BOB DYLAN

**❝To be one, to be united is a great thing. But to respect the right to be different is maybe even greater.❞** BONO

**❝**I can't remember sacrifices at this stage of the game.**❞**
KEITH RICHARDS

**❝Too many people are obsessed with pop. The position of rock'n'roll in our subculture has become far too important especially in the delving for philosophical content.❞** MICK JAGGER

**❝**We wouldn't have been able to handle the fame if it would've hit us all of a sudden. When I was young I always dreamed of having a group that was adored by few and ignored by the rest of the world, like Nick Drake. Fortunately, when we became famous, I had no time to reflect upon anything any more.**❞** ROBERT SMITH, THE CURE

**❝In the end, you become part of everything you hate, basically.❞** RAY DAVIES, THE KINKS

**❝**I'm much more comfortable with doing interviews now because I'm harder to misquote. Everything I'm about is freedom of choice and knowing what the truth can do.**❞**
PRINCE

**❝The only thing that stands up is whether you've got it or not. The only thing that counts is if you're still around. And I'm still around.❞** VAN MORRISON

**❝**Let's face it, you can't worship a guy for destroying an instrument in the name of rock.**❞** PETE TOWNSHEND, THE WHO

**I think that cynicism is a positive value. You have to be cynical. You can't not be cynical. The more people I have encouraged to be cynical, the better job I've done.**
FRANK ZAPPA

I believe that music should communicate to as many people as you can get to. In that kind of DJ, music journalist world the snobbery comes from 'it's too successful, therefore I can't like it. It's too big a hit'.
**MICK HUCKNALL, SIMPLY RED**

**There isn't a single name punk musician who doesn't have some skeleton in his cupboard – even if it's only education.** TONY JAMES, SIGUE SIGUE SPUTNIK

All we're presenting is viewpoints, some of which are very narrow, but they're just as valid because they're just opinions. **TINA WEYMOUTH, TALKING HEADS**

**We thought that we had the answers, it was the questions we had wrong.** BONO

Better compare us with President Carter, because people vote the same way as they buy records. **ACE FREHLEY, KISS**

**I've dressed in women's clothes, I've dressed as a Nazi, I've gone on stage naked, I've gone on so drunk I didn't even know I did a show. I've done so many stupid things, but it's all part of Ozzy. I never pre-planned 99.9 percent of the things I've done. Some were drastically wrong, some were drastically right.** OZZY OSBOURNE

Non-violence is a flop. The only bigger flop is violence.
JOAN BAEZ

**Message songs, as everybody knows, are a drag. It's only college newspaper editors and single**

girls under fourteen that could possibly have time for them. " BOB DYLAN

# "CONVICTS ARE THE BEST AUDIENCES I EVER PLAYED FOR." JOHNNY CASH

" I think it's great because Who's Who is an American institution and I believe in anything that is an American institution, such as Hugh Hefner, Walt Disney, the Boy Scouts and Budweiser. "

ALICE COOPER, BORN VINCENT FURNIER, ON HIS INCLUSION IN 'WHO'S WHO IN AMERICA'

" We were scamming the world. How on earth could anyone think that we deserved to be this huge band ... Have you seen us live? It was funny. All of that – MTV, magazines, critics' choice – was all irrelevant. All that was important was the three of us playing music. And I don't think we wrote one bad song. Everything we did when we were together was fucking great. " DAVE GROHL, NIRVANA

" Living in New York is like coming all the time. "
GENE SIMMONS, KISS

" I do believe in equality, but I also believe in distance. "
BOB DYLAN

" The things we've tried to achieve in the past by flashing a V-sign, we will now try through wishing. "
JOHN LENNON AND YOKO ONO, AD IN THE NEW YORK TIMES, 1979

" We don't have a manifesto or a set of principles. We just make it up as we go along. " ALEX TURNER, ARCTIC MONKEYS

" Pop is actually my least favourite kind of music, because it lacks real depth. " CHRISTINA AGUILERA

"I'D RATHER THE MAFIA THAN DECCA." KEITH RICHARDS

# CHAPTER FOUR
# THE BUSINESS OF MUSIC

❝ Decca are supposed to be making records, but they might just as easily be making baked beans. A record, to them, is just a piece of plastic and what's on there doesn't really matter. ❞ KEITH RICHARDS

❝ To me, the music industry has got about as much meaning as a comic book. ❞ VAN MORRISON

❝ I've given them a lot of control – I made the music because I know how to do that, but then for the promotional side I stepped back and thought, 'I've got to trust this lot, because I've never done this before'. That was the wrongest thing I could have done. All they know how to do is what's already been done and I don't want to do anything that's already been done. ❞ AMY WINEHOUSE

❝ We know that Sony completely own us. They can do anything they want with us, they can drop us. In fact, they said if you want you can come in and smash the place up, it would make good press. It wouldn't be good press – we'd end up paying for it. ❞ RICHEY EDWARDS, MANIC STREET PREACHERS

❝ Make sure you stay ordinary. ❞ LEE EASTMAN, ADVISING HIS SON-IN-LAW PAUL McCARTNEY

> **"**We have no approval on the scripts – all we have approval on is the money.**"**
>
> **COLONEL TOM PARKER, ON THE APPALLING PRESLEY MOVIES**

> **"I think Australians are down to earth... We have a good work ethic, and that can only be helpful in this industry."** KYLIE MINOGUE

> **"**Next time you go out for dinner, have a look around the table and if everyone is on your payroll, the chances are you have become a prick.**"** BONO

> **"I didn't want to find a horse's head in my bed."**
>
> PAUL ANKA, EXPLAINING WHY HE GAVE 'MY WAY' TO FRANK SINATRA

> **"**I never had the feeling I ever had to make a dime doing anything.**"** RICK RUBIN, DEF AMERICAN RECORDS

> **"When I got the famous haircut of 1974 or whenever, everyone said 'Oh God, what did you do? You were so perfect, two brothers who had that sort of long curly hair- great gimmick!' And no-one would look me in the eye. Our manager was really upset. It was like I had murdered my mother or something."** RON MAEL, SPARKS

> **"**The whole business is built on ego, vanity, self-satisfaction, and it's total crap to pretend it's not.**"**
>
> **GEORGE MICHAEL**

> **"The music industry has gotten so it's like Vietnam. A lot of guys making a lot of money, some guys getting cut up, and in five years ain't much of it going to be worth a pinch of shit."** LEVON HELM, THE BAND

> **"**You've gotta be business savvy really, or else you get the piss taken out of you.**" MELANIE B, SPICE GIRLS**

**Why should I tell the truth if it makes us look like schmucks in comparison to a liar? I didn't write the rules, I just live by them.**

IRVING AZOFF, MANAGER OF THE EAGLES

The key to building a superstar is to keep their mouth shut. To reveal an artist to the people can be to destroy him. It isn't to anyone's advantage to see the truth. In the long run the audience matters more. That's the story.

**BOB EZRIN, PRODUCER**

**In an industry riddled with drug addicts, homosexuals and hangers-on, I am one of the few real men left.**

DON ARDEN, SOMETIME MANAGER OF SMALL FACES,
AMEN CORNER, THE MOVE, ELO ETC.

If you can survive in this line of work, then you can survive in the jungle. I know I'm a mixed character, but it's horses for courses. If someone's being rough with you, you gotta be rough back. **PETER GRANT, MANAGER OF LED ZEPPELIN**

**When you get in the record business, someone gonna rip you anyway so that don't bother me. If you don't rip me, she gonna rip me, and if she don't rip me, he gonna rip me, so I'm gonna get ripped, so you don't be bothered by that, because people round you gonna rip you if they can.** MUDDY WATERS

Record company presidents tried to create power pop because they couldn't look like punks. They couldn't change their haircuts because they didn't have any hair.

**BILLY IDOL**

**American music is something the rest of the world wants to listen to. Our job is to make sure they pay for it.** JASON BERMAN, RIAA

❝Sure I lie, but it's more like... tinting. It's all just negotiating theatrics.❞ **IRVING AZOFF, MANAGER OF THE EAGLES**

❝**You can't go beyond your limitations. They want me to try an artistic picture. That's fine, maybe I can pull it off one day. But not now. I've done eleven pictures and they've all made money. A certain type of audience like me. I entertain them with what I'm doing. I'd be a fool to tamper with that kind of success.**❞ ELVIS PRESLEY

❝All those shoe salesmen who ran the music business really felt threatened by our very existence. But I never like that Communist image from the outset, 'cos me being Jewish for one thing, I really hate those Commie bastards.❞ **SYLVAIN SYLVAIN, NEW YORK DOLLS**

❝**I want to manage those four boys. It wouldn't take me more than two half-days a week.**❞
BRIAN EPSTEIN, NOVEMBER 9, 1961

❝**I NEVER GOT INTO HIP-HOP FOR THE MUSIC. I GOT INTO IT FOR THE BUSINESS.**❞ **50 CENT**

❝**My job is to get that emotion into a record. We deal with the young generation, with people lacking identification, the disassociated, the kids who feel they don't belong, who are in the 'in-between' period in their lives.**❞
PHIL SPECTOR

❝The mainstream music business is such a bunch of fucking retards as far as I'm concerned.❞
**THOM YORKE, RADIOHEAD**

**❝I shall consider it my patriotic duty to keep Elvis in the ninety per cent tax bracket.❞** COLONEL TOM PARKER

**❝**The trouble is that so much of the record business is being run by people who don't have a clue what it's about. **❞**
PAUL McCARTNEY

SIMON LE BON

**❝I read the phrase 'New Romantic' in NME and I really liked it, so I put it in 'Planet Earth'. I never intended it to be a name for a movement. ❞**

SIMON LE BON, DURAN DURAN

**❝**It wasn't so much that Brian Epstein discovered The Beatles but that The Beatles discovered Brian Epstein. **❞**
**PAUL McCARTNEY**

**❝Money had never been the main thing for me. It's the legacy that was important. ❞** BERRY GORDY, MOTOWN RECORDS

**❝**They all hate each other deep down, but they're not gonna say it on camera. **❞** SIMON COWELL, ON AMERICAN IDOL

**❝I knew Roy Orbison's voice was pure gold, but I felt he'd be dead inside a month if people saw him. ❞**
SAM PHILLIPS, SUN RECORDS

**❝**These boys won't make it. Groups with guitars and drums are out. Go back to Liverpool, Mr. Epstein, you have a good business there. **❞**
**VERDICT OF THE BEATLES' FIRST RECORD AUDITION IN LONDON**

**❝I'd like to live up to my reputation of being a nice guy.❞**
COLONEL TOM PARKER

**❝**By the mid-1970s, rock music will be San Francisco's fifth largest industry, led only by construction, finance, insurance and manufacturing.**❞**
**MICHAEL PHILLIPS, VICE PRESIDENT OF THE BANK OF CALIFORNIA, 1969**

**❝**I never signed a contract with The Beatles. I had given my word about what I intended to do and that was enough. I abided by the terms and no-one ever worried about me not signing it. **❞ BRIAN EPSTEIN**

EDDIE VEDDER

**❝Actually, we're a complete fraud. We can't sing, play or write songs, we get other people to do it for us. We also pay radio stations lots of money to tell kids to buy our records and wear clothes like us. ❞** EDDIE VEDDER, PEARL JAM

**❝**The last official get-together I had with The Monkees was when they gave me a six-dollar watch, upon my retirement from the group. They all chipped in and even had it engraved. It read 'To Peter, from all the guys at work.' **❞ PETER TORK, THE MONKEES**

**❝Island Records have got gold records on the wall like other people have china ducks. ❞** RICHARD THOMPSON

**❝**When I first knew Elvis, he had a million dollars worth of talent. Now he has a million dollars. **❞ COLONEL TOM PARKER**

> **I think all revolutions are meaningless, especially those led by CBS and EMI.** BOB GELDOF

> Running a record company hardly seems a sensible thing for a grown man to be doing.
> **MAURICE OBERSTEIN, HEAD OF CBS RECORDS UK**

> **I never knew a musician who wasn't more concerned about money than I was.** MILES COPELAND, POLICE MANAGER

> He's going to take your money, but he tells you. It's dead honest, that.
> **KAY CARROLL, MANAGER OF THE FALL, ON MILES COPELAND**

> **I drove The Beach Boys through the wall. When they were exhausted, I drove them harder, because they asked for it.**
> MURRY WILSON, FATHER OF BRIAN, CARL AND DENNIS WILSON

> The big beat, cars and young love. It was a trend and we jumped on it. **LEONARD CHESS, ON CHESS RECORDS' LAUNCH OF CHUCK BERRY'S 'MAYBELLINE', IN 1955**

> **A lot of us executives are walking around physically ill – needing to pretend that we're creating something artistically worthy... But since we're all capitalist enterprises, we have to capture the lowest common denominator. What's wrong is that we have to cater to the rancid, infantile, pubescent tastes of the public.**
> JERRY WEXLER, SENIOR VICE PRESIDENT OF WARNER BROTHERS.

> Some people believe we are doing this for the money, but we aren't. It's fun – the money comes with it.
> **STIG ANDERSON, ABBA MANAGER**

❝If you hype something and it succeeds, you're a genius and it wasn't a hype. If you hype it and it fails, it's just a hype.❞ NEIL BOGART, PRESIDENT CASABLANCA RECORDS

❝Warner Brothers is the only company that gives you a manual of where to go after gigs: nightclubs, bars, and the local VD clinic.❞ PHIL LYNOTT, THIN LIZZY

❝We tried to create a situation where the kids would be more interested in creating havoc than in buying records.❞ MALCOLM McLAREN, MANAGER, SEX PISTOLS

❝Christ, if the people bought the records for the music, this thing would have died a death long ago.❞ MALCOLM McLAREN, MANAGER, SEX PISTOLS

❝Every record can be a hit if you concentrate on it enough.❞ PHIL SPECTOR

❝What most people don't realise is that the whole thing is about getting as much money as possible in as short a time as possible with as much style as possible.❞ MALCOLM McLAREN, MANAGER OF THE SEX PISTOLS

❝IN LOS ANGELES, THEY DON'T WANT YOU TO FAIL, THEY WANT YOU TO DIE.❞ DAVID GEFFEN

❝I gave The Beatles their first tour – I took them to Hamburg before they ever made a record, I gave Mick Jagger his first tour in this country. James Brown was with me. I put Joe Tex in the business.❞ LITTLE RICHARD

**"I don't suppose agents will mind me saying that they think people are more or less like cattle."**

RAY DAVIES, THE KINKS

"Like many artists, my deal meant I paid for the cost of recording the music. I paid for the marketing. I don't know any other business where you pay for something and then someone else owns it." **MICK HUCKNALL, SIMPLY RED**

**"What people in America don't understand is that the music they heard was not Them but session men... I was forced to perform under these circumstances."**

VAN MORRISON

KURT COBAIN

**"I wish there had been a music business 101 course I could have taken."** **KURT COBAIN**

**"I'd rather try and close a deal with the Devil."**

HAL WALLIS, PRODUCER OF NINE PRESLEY PICTURES, ON COLONEL TOM PARKER

"You can always come back, but you've got to come back better. If you come back worse, or even the same, you're dead." **PHIL SPECTOR**

**"I think all kids are anarchists until they get dragged into the system."** MALCOLM McLAREN, MANAGER, SEX PISTOLS

"WHAT WILL I BE DOING IN TWENTY YEARS' TIME? I'LL BE DEAD, DARLING! ARE YOU CRAZY?" FREDDIE MERCURY, QUEEN

# CHAPTER FIVE
# SPEAKING WORDS OF WISDOM

“ Americans want grungy people, stabbing themselves in the head on stage. They get a bright bunch like us, with deodorant on, they don't get it. ” LIAM GALLAGHER, OASIS

“ I would rather eat my own testicles than reform The Smiths, and that's saying something for a vegetarian. ” MORRISSEY

“ I'm quite sure that if I wasn't in a group I'd be locked up. ” PHIL LYNOTT, THIN LIZZY

“ We're not claiming to be soul divas, we're just having a laugh! ” VICTORIA BECKHAM, SPICE GIRLS

“ We live in this little bubble, which is not really a good representation of everyday life. It's incredible, we're pampered little babies. We're spoilt brats. We're rich pompous rock stars who stay in big fancy hotels and smoke cigars and drink wine... ” CHAD SMITH, RED HOT CHILI PEPPERS

“ I wanted to be the rock Tony Newley. I've never been convinced that I'm a musician. ” DAVID BOWIE

“ If you wanna save the planet, jump up and down! ” MADONNA AT LIVE EARTH

**There is nothing fake about how I look now. I had already thought about toning my look in The Spice Girls but people wanted to see Ginger Spice in a bustier and big boots.** GERI HALLIWELL

**We're only in it for the volume.**
TERRY 'GEEZER' BUTLER, BLACK SABBATH

**Nobody can pretend their shit don't stink.**
TINA WEYMOUTH, TALKING HEADS

**It doesn't matter how you travel it, it's the same road. It doesn't get any easier when you get bigger, it gets harder. And it will kill you if you let it.** JAMES BROWN

It's been a long haul and I've done everything there is to do. But for the most part I wonder why have I come through after what I did and others didn't? Some genuine, nice guys didn't make it and then there's me, who's been boozing and snorting coke all his life, still swanning around. **OZZY OSBOURNE**

**I guess I am a feminist of sorts. I love women so much, and I celebrate the feminine in me because I appreciate it so much.** STEVEN TYLER

I only write about stuff that's happened to me - stuff I can't get past personally. Luckily, I'm quite self-destructive.
AMY WINEHOUSE

**I wouldn't exist as a musician without the tape-recorder. More than anything else, that is the instrument I play.** BRIAN ENO

"As far as the press is concerned, they're going to say what they want to say. Probably about 10-15 per cent of the time it's accurate." **JUSTIN TIMBERLAKE**

**One day Neil Young will write a happy song, but I'll probably sell it to TV for a commercial.** NEIL YOUNG

"There's more important people who can have an opinion. Why does it make us have an opinion because we're in a band?"

**MATT HELDERS, THE ARCTIC MONKEYS, ON THE LIVE EARTH CONCERTS/GLOBAL WARMING**

# "ME AND JANET REALLY ARE TWO DIFFERENT PEOPLE." MICHAEL JACKSON

"If a guy does some great things, then even his down moments are interesting. You can't live your life without pressure periods." **PAUL McCARTNEY**

**Celebrity and secrets don't go together. The bastards will get you in the end.** GEORGE MICHAEL

"I don't really know what I am, or where I'm from. I just know I'm not from here." **MARC BOLAN**

**In the early days, we just wore black onstage. Very bold, my dear. Then we introduced white, for variety, and it simply grew and grew.** FREDDIE MERCURY, QUEEN

"We never thought of ourselves as a 'heavy metal band' we've always regarded ourselves as a rock band. But every now and again it does come on like a sledge hammer." **ANGUS YOUNG, AC/DC**

**I would rather retain the position of being a photostat machine with an image, because I think most songwriters are anyway.** DAVID BOWIE

People think The Beatles know what's going on. We don't. We're just doing it. JOHN LENNON

**If you haven't got The Beatles by now, you're not going to get it.** LIAM GALLAGHER, OASIS

New rave will save me. I like the idea of going to a gig and getting a few glowsticks out. **MATT BELLAMY, MUSE**

**There are any number of ways to get from one place to another on the neck of the guitar that I don't know about.** TOM VERLAINE, TELEVISION

We are robots. We have become robots through our experience of working and living. We are just musical workers. **FLORIAN SCHNEIDER, KRAFTWERK**

# "SO, WHERE'S THE CANNES FILM FESTIVAL BEING HELD THIS YEAR?"

CHRISTINA AGUILERA

I'm just another gullible youth; I'm into idols. **PAUL WELLER, THE JAM**

**There's a party in my mind and I hope it never stops.** DAVID BYRNE, TALKING HEADS

I would say you need to be very centred, and spiritually know where you're at, all the time. Don't read the tabloids. Don't be obsessed with what people are writing or saying... It took me a long time to acknowledge that my personal feelings mattered. **MARIAH CAREY**

**"I needed a name in a hurry and I picked that one."** BOB DYLAN

**"I never work on anything. Dedication is such a weird word after all, after Albert Schweitzer and people like that. That's dedication, when you give your whole life. No-one dedicates themselves to anything now."** RINGO STARR

**"I like to be extremely forthright and not say anything at all."** IAN DURY

**"All I've had to do is stand in the background, sometimes put on a bit of make-up, and look happy to be there."** BILL WYMAN, THE ROLLING STONES

**"When I get up in the morning, I listen to Vivaldi and Marvin Gaye's Greatest Hits."** MICK JAGGER

**"'Blue Suede Shoes' was the easiest song I ever wrote. Got up at 3.00am when me and my wife Velda were living in a government project in Jackson, Tennessee. Had the idea in my head, seeing kids by the bandstand so proud of their new city shoes – you gotta be real poor to care about new shoes like I did – and that morning I went downstairs and wrote out the words on a potato sack. We didn't have any reason to have writing paper around."** CARL PERKINS

**"We've always had a wild image. We built ourselves on the fact. Groups like The Hollies envy our image."** BRIAN JONES, THE ROLLING STONES

**"I'm not in love with music. You've got to play around with it, or it gets to be a dreadful bore."** DAVID BOWIE

**"I've had enough of being perceived as a doomy Goth casualty."** ROBERT SMITH, THE CURE

❝I enjoy life. I think I'll enjoy death even more. Life is too confusing.❞ **CAT STEVENS**

❝**Every year when I open a new diary, Easter Week is crossed off. My manager knows I'll be away camping then.**❞ CLIFF RICHARD

❝I think I must be a victim of circumstance, really. Most of it's my own doing; I'm a victim of my own practical jokes. I suppose that reflects a rather selfish attitude. I like to be the recipient of my own doings. Nine time out of ten, I am. I set traps and fall into them.❞ **KEITH MOON**

❝**I'm not a paedophile – I came to Cambodia because I read a book about the Mekong.**❞ GARY GLITTER

❝When I left school, I took off my school uniform and put on a hippie uniform instead. My new double album, **Incantations,** is a load of rubbish really. There are a couple of parts in which I'm expressing myself completely, not using irrelevant stupid things like emotions. The rest is rubbish.❞ **MIKE OLDFIELD**

❝**What would I have become if I hadn't joined the Stones? A layabout, but a very high-class one.**❞ KEITH RICHARDS

❝I follow a gentleman's pursuits.❞ **MICK JAGGER**

❝**I'm not a superstar, I started life as a chubby kid and things never got much better.**❞ DAVID CROSBY

❝I wouldn't go out surfing. I was scared of the water it really scared me.❞ **BRIAN WILSON, BEACH BOYS**

❝**There was a big rumour at Newport in 1965 that I cried when I was booed. I didn't know enough to.**❞ BOB DYLAN

**❝**Nobody in this business is very stable, else we wouldn't all be up on stages making arses of ourselves.**❞**
**KRIS KRISTOFFERSON**

**❝We're intellectual twelve year olds.❞** TOMMY RAMONE

**❝**We were a band who made it very big, that's all. Our best work was never recorded.**❞ JOHN LENNON**

**❝I was just a hired guitar player when we started.❞**
KEITH RICHARDS

**❝**I tried to commit suicide one day. It was a very Woody Allen type suicide. I turned on the gas and left all the windows open.**❞ ELTON JOHN**

**❝I feel like an actor when I'm on stage, rather than a rock artist. I very rarely have felt like a rock artist. I don't think that's much of a vocation, being a rock'n'roller.❞**
DAVID BOWIE

**❝**I can't help it if I've never looked healthy.**❞**
**KEITH RICHARDS**

**❝I never wanted to be a great star. I just wanted to go on stage and be a great musician.❞** STEVE WINWOOD

**❝**I've got to write songs. But if I had to do something else I'd like to be an osteopath. I'd like to cure arthritis and make people's bones work.**❞**
**RAY DAVIES, THE KINKS**

RAY DAVIES

MICK JAGGER

**"The trouble with me is that I have to be kicked up the arse, but there's no-one who can do it."** MICK JAGGER

**"**I go to bed all right; I wake up twisted.**"** **RAY DAVIES, THE KINKS**

**"Starvation in India doesn't worry me one bit. Not one iota, it doesn't man. And it doesn't worry you, if you're honest. You just pose. You don't even know it exists. You've just seen the charity ads. You can't pretend to me that an ad reached down into the depths of your soul and actually makes you feel more for these people than, for instance, you feel about getting a new car."** PAUL McCARTNEY

**"**I manage to look so young because I'm mentally retarded.**"** **DEBBIE HARRY, BLONDIE**

**"I don't call myself a poet, because I don't like the word. I'm a trapeze artist."** BOB DYLAN

**"**The only Maybelline I knew was the name of a cow.**"** **CHUCK BERRY**

**"The image we have would be hard for Mickey Mouse to maintain."** KAREN CARPENTER

**"**I'm just part of the whole music-hall tradition.**"** **BILLY IDOL**

**"My ultimate vocation in life is to be an irritant."** ELVIS COSTELLO

**"** I'm all for these sociological lyrics; I just can't be bothered to write them. **"** SUGGS, MADNESS

**" My music has a high irritation factor. You can't put it on and eat potato chips to it and invite the neighbours in for a barbecue. It's got 'prick' in it, and 'wop' and 'I'm gonna take off my pants'. I entertain, but I've got something to say. "** RANDY NEWMAN

**"** What's wrong with coffee tables? Millions of people have got coffee tables. What's wrong with having a book on there and a Simply Red and a Sade CD? I don't have a problem with it. **"** MICK HUCKNALL, SIMPLY RED

**" I'm proud of the group and name, but I think the clean American thing hurt us. "** BRIAN WILSON, BEACH BOYS

**"** I didn't really want to become a hit pop writer... I would have loved to have been the guy who thought up **The Guinness Book Of Records**. **"** TIM RICE

# " WE ALWAYS MAKE OUR MISTAKES IN PUBLIC. " PAUL McCARTNEY

**"** We have taken the perspiration out of drumming. It is no longer like chopping wood. We have electronic percussion. Our drummers no longer sweat. **"**
**RALF HUTTER, KRAFTWERK**

**" Success always necessitates a degree of ruthlessness. Given the choice of friendship or success, I'd probably choose success. "** STING

**"** 'My Generation' was our biggest seller and we never hope or want to produce anything like it again. **"**
**PETE TOWNSHEND, THE WHO**

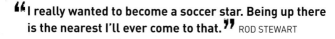

**I really wanted to become a soccer star. Being up there is the nearest I'll ever come to that.** ROD STEWART

I don't like to be called Elvis the Pelvis... I mean, it's one of the most childish expressions I ever heard coming from an adult. But, uh, if they want to call me that, I mean there's nothing I can do about it. **ELVIS PRESLEY**

**I just happened to have the tape on the wrong way 'round. It just blew my mind. The voice sounds like an old Indian.**

JOHN LENNON ON THE FIRST USE OF REVERSE TAPES ON 'RAIN', 1966

I'm not kidding myself. My voice alone is just an ordinary voice. What people come to see is how I use it. If I stand still while I'm singing, I'm dead, man. I might as well go back to driving a truck. **ELVIS PRESLEY, 1956**

# I'M AN INSTANT STAR; JUST ADD WATER AND STIR. DAVID BOWIE

I never get embarrassed on stage. Never. Never, because if you fall right on your ass it doesn't matter. I've fallen over onstage numerous times, and you always just kind of go, 'oh well' and get back up.
**JOHNNY BORRELL, RAZORLIGHT**

**I was always a freak. Never a hippie, but always a freak** FRANK ZAPPA

My voice is like a house I'm keeping up. You don't just build a house and do nothing else to it. You're always washing the window, painting, adding a room.
**RAY CHARLES**

**" I'm sort of out there in the middle somewhere, without any category. "**
EMMYLOU HARRIS

**"** I must say, I really don't like singing very much. I'm not really a good enough singer to really enjoy it, but I am getting into it a little bit. **"**
**MICK JAGGER**

**" Getting myself up in the morning, or should I say afternoon, is like picking at a scab. "** JANIS JOPLIN

JANIS JOPLIN

**"** We're Pat Boone, only a little cleaner. **"** **RICHARD CARPENTER**

**" I'm weird, I really don't play a lot. Most people think that I probably go home to some guitar shop in the sky and practice all day. "** JEFF BECK

**"** The big difference between us and punk groups is that we like KC & The Sunshine Band. You ask Johnny Rotten if he likes KC & The Sunshine Band and he'll blow snot in your face. **"** **CHRIS FRANTZ, TALKING HEADS**

**❝I've met all the women and I'll tell you – I'm more woman than any of them. I'm a real woman because I have love, dependability, I'm good, kind, gentle and I have the power to give real love. Why else would you think that such a strong man as David Bowie would be close to me? He's a real man and I'm a real woman. Just like Catherine Deneuve❞** IGGY POP

❝We chose the name because it represents something really cheap'n'nasty.❞ **JEREMY VALENTINE, THE CORTINAS**

**❝Just dig the noise and you've got our sound. We're musical primitives.❞** JOHN CALE, VELVET UNDERGROUND, 1966

❝One of my dreams was to open for the Stones. Now all I want to do is open for Rimbaud.❞
**PATTI SMITH**

**❝I hang my laundry on the line when I write.❞**
JONI MITCHELL

❝We're just a bunch of crummy musicians really.❞
**GEORGE HARRISON, RADIO INTERVIEW, 1962**

GEORGE HARRISON

**We always knew something would happen sooner or later. We always had this blind Bethlehem star ahead, of us. Fame is what everyone wants, in some form or another.** PAUL McCARTNEY

If I hadn't been a songwriter, I'd have liked to have written children's fairy stories. **ROY WOOD**

**I don't exactly identify with Dracula, but I sympathise.**
DAVE VANIAN, THE DAMNED

We only knew four chords, but we arranged them pretty well.
**LEMMY, MOTÖRHEAD, ON DAYS WITH SPACE-ROCKERS HAWKWIND**

## I'VE ALWAYS LOOKED LIKE A BANK CLERK WHO'S FREAKED OUT. ELTON JOHN

We consider ourselves synthetic beings. We cannot speak for David Bowie but it certainly shows from his work. He is what we call a liquid personality.
**FLORIAN SCHNEIDER, KRAFTWERK**

**Nobody notices me. Nobody thinks I'm me. But then I look less like me than most of the people coming to our concerts.** ROBERT SMITH, THE CURE

"ELVIS DIED WHEN HE WENT INTO THE ARMY."

JOHN LENNON

# CHAPTER SIX
# HOPE I DIE BEFORE I GET OLD

**" We know a lot of people don't like us because they say we're scruffy and don't wash. So what? They don't have to come and look at us, do they? If they don't like me, they can keep away. "** MICK JAGGER, 1964

**"** When I come back from touring I'm shocked to find a lot of my mates tend to be going to bed far too early, and that means I should probably be doing the same. Maybe I should stop having a good time and get old. **"** ROBERT PLANT

**" I despise those cunts. The Stones should have quit in 1965. You never see any of these cunts walking down the street. If it gets so you can't see us that way, I don't want it. "** SID VICIOUS

**"** I think... those pieces of plastic we did are still some of the finest pieces of plastic around. **"**
**RINGO STARR, THE BEATLES**

**" All you've got to do is delete the words 'punk rock' and write in Rolling Stones and you've got the same press as you had fifteen years ago... they've made the press play the same old games as they played with us. They puked at London Airport, we pissed in the filling station. "**
KEITH RICHARDS

**❝**I'd rather be dead than singing 'Satisfaction' when I'm forty-five.**❞** MICK JAGGER

**❝I used to admire Metallica and I don't wanna see them going to fucking therapy. I don't wanna see these fragile fucking old men that can't have a cocktail any more because they're afraid of what they'll become. Fuck that!❞** KERRY KING, SLAYER

**❝**I smash guitars because I like them. I usually smash a guitar when it's at its best.**❞** PETE TOWNSHEND, THE WHO, 1965

**❝They say we are obscene and vulgar... but I don't let them hang us up... we just get excited by the music and carried away.❞** JIMI HENDRIX

**❝**We like to look sixteen and bored shitless.**❞** DAVID JOHANSEN, NEW YORK DOLLS

**❝When my time comes, I hope I fall dead in the middle of the stage and I hope it's to a song I wrote.❞** DOLLY PARTON

**❝**A midlife crisis is a man buying a Corvette... a man buying a Lamborghini has no crisis.**❞** REVEREND RUN, RUN-DMC

**❝We like this kind of music. Jazz is strictly for the stay-at-homes.❞** BUDDY HOLLY

**❝**The problem with all those people relating to 'Satisfaction' is that they want to drag you back. Or they want you to drag them back, which is worse.**❞** KEITH RICHARDS

**❝We still have the code of the street.❞** MICK JONES, THE CLASH

**❝**You know something – I really hate feeling too old to be doing what I'm doing.**❞** PETE TOWNSHEND, THE WHO

**Gram Parsons had it all sussed. He didn't stick around. He made his best work and then he died. That's the way I'm going to do it. I'm never going to stick around long enough to churn out a load of mediocre crap like those guys from the Sixties.** ELVIS COSTELLO

We're hoping to retire when all our kids get to about 16 and 17. Dave [Gahan]'s kids and Martin [Gore]'s kids are all similar ages. We'll retire and get out of the limelight, and we could have a whole new, young Depeche Mode coming out in a few years. **ANDREW FLETCHER, DEPECHE MODE**

ANDREW FLETCHER

**I was around in the early Seventies and you needed a fucking GCE in playing the guitar. You had to be Eric Clapton before you could get a deal, it was ridiculous. Then these punks came in and blew everything apart.**

PHIL LYNOTT, THIN LIZZY

My brother Dennis came home from school one day and he said 'Listen, you guys, it looks like surfing's going to be the next big craze and you guys ought to write a song about it.' Because, at that time, we were writing songs for friends and school assemblies. **BRIAN WILSON, THE BEACH BOYS**

PETE TOWNSHEND

**"The first couple of times I saw the group, I must say, I didn't like them, but I got used to them, although it took some time. But then, I guess the first time some people taste champagne, they want to spit it out, right?"**

NOEL HYMAN,
FATHER OF JOEY RAMONE

**"I'm no punk anymore, if I ever was. I always stood outside looking in, and always will."**
**PETE TOWNSHEND, THE WHO**

**"Hippies? Why, I'm the original."** JERRY LEE LEWIS

**"**Our music is the answer to the early Seventies. That was bullshit. We play rock'n'roll. We don't do solos.**"**
**JOEY RAMONE**

**"If any of them punk rockers goes anywhere near my kit I shall kick them square in the knackers. I got fifteen years in this bloody business and what do these bastards know?"** KEITH MOON

**"**I give the Stones about another two years. I'm saving for the future. I bank all my song royalties, for a start.**"**
**MICK JAGGER, 1964**

**"Lots of people who complained about us receiving the MBE received theirs for heroism in the war – for killing**

people. We received ours for entertaining other people.
I'd say we deserved ours more, wouldn't you? "
JOHN LENNON

" I'm a time traveller. To me, it's all still 1970. I've been
moving backwards at the speed of light. I think the punk
rock thing is rubbish. " IAN ANDERSON, JETHRO TULL

" The old are scared of us. They don't want the change.
It makes them irrelevant to what's going on now and
they know it. " JOHNNY ROTTEN, SEX PISTOLS

" Whatever I do, it's my business. It's not my job to
parent America. " CHRISTINA AGUILERA

## "OUR CHILDREN WILL HATE US TOO, YOU KNOW." JOHN LENNON

" I see my exit as something like being run over by a bus.
But I'm deadly serious about this: I'm not going to be
around to witness my artistic decline. " ELVIS COSTELLO

" We were the youngest generation of moneyed people,
and we were just bigger kids about it. "
MAMA CASS ELLIOT, THE MAMAS & THE PAPAS

" I ain't never lived under five floors up. "
MICK JONES, THE CLASH

" They may be world famous, but four shrieking monkeys
are not going to use a privileged family name without
permission. " FRAU EVA VON ZEPPELIN ON LED ZEPPELIN

" A lot of people start to fall to bits at thirty – that's why it's
dangerous. I don't fall to bits at all. Quite honestly, once
you are able to reproduce, you're over the hill. You start to
go downhill at eighteen, physically. " MICK JAGGER

**I'm in my thirties, I'm not only part of the Establishment, I am the Establishment.** PETE TOWNSHEND, THE WHO

It does seem ironic that people moan about me not shaving and not combing my hair, when two years ago, it you didn't have a wash you were hailed as a prophet. **PETE SHELLEY, BUZZCOCKS**

# IT'S THE OLD PHILOSOPHY: IF I'M TOO LOUD FOR YOU, YOU'RE TOO OLD FOR ME. STIV BATORS, DEAD BOYS

I don't really want to talk about the Pistols. It's depressing. It's morbid. It happened, and that's all. **JOHN LYDON, ERSTWHILE JOHNNY ROTTEN**

**More traffic accidents are caused by classic rock radio than by drink driving – because people are falling asleep at the wheel through total boredom because they play the same old songs over and over again!** IAN GILLAN, DEEP PURPLE

For one night in the States, I earned more than my old man did in his entire working life. **JIM CAPALDI, TRAFFIC**

**I'm thirty-two now, and I think, shit, I must be a bit more mature. But I'm not. Still gullible for long legs and a big tit.** ROD STEWART

I don't have a love affair with the guitar – I don't polish it after every performance. I play the fucking thing. **PETE TOWNSHEND, THE WHO**

**"**We had gone as far as we could go. Everyone was trying to turn us into a big group and I hated that. They wanted to make us into another version of The Rolling Stones. **"**

JOHN LYDON, ON THE SEX PISTOLS' DEMISE

**"**I don't know you very well, and I am not a bullshitter. I get that you don't like the album. You're 80; you're not supposed to like my album. **"**

KELLY CLARKSON ON LABEL BOSS CLIVE DAVIS NOT LIKING HER NEW ALBUM

**"**I was unfaithful in the early days but not now. I still get women throwing themselves at me but I feel like a bit of a dick when some 21-year old bimbo comes on to me – I mean, I'm 53. **"** OZZY OSBOURNE

OZZY OSBOURNE

**"**You know, everybody makes a big deal about the Sixties. The Sixties, it's like the Civil War days. But, I mean, you're talking to a person who owns the Sixties. Did I ever want to acquire the Sixties? No. But I own the Sixties – who's going to argue with me?... I'll give 'em to you if you want 'em. You can have 'em. **"** BOB DYLAN

"IF I SEEM FREE, IT'S BECAUSE I'M ALWAYS RUNNING."

JIMI HENDRIX

# CHAPTER SEVEN
# DON'T LET ME BE MISUNDERSTOOD

**"**I believe that instinct is what makes a genius a genius.**"**
BOB DYLAN

**"**A minor is one of my all-time favourite keys to play in. It's a very moody key, and also A is the first letter of my name. It just represents the songs through my eyes. **"** **ALICIA KEYS**

**"I've always spent more time with a smile on my face than not, but the thing is, I don't write about it. "**
ROBERT SMITH, THE CURE

**"**We just write down a bunch of words and pray to God they make sense. And if we don't, it doesn't matter, we're artists. **" TOM DELONGE, BLINK 182**

**"I want to be a poet. I don't want to talk about genies in bottles anymore. "** CHRISTINA AGUILERA

**"**I'm very misunderstood, you know. It's the price I have to pay. Beethoven and Michelangelo were misunderstood in their time, to. I'm not concerned about now, but when I leave this earth, I'll be appreciated. **" MARVIN GAYE**

**"To write I have to feel slightly sorry for myself... my best songs come when I have that feeling that I've left the party early. "** CHRIS MARTIN, COLDPLAY

My name is no big deal. It's meaningless. I tried to get rid of the burden of the Bob Dylan myth for a long time.
**BOB DYLAN**

**I get people coming up on the streets in Oxford saying, 'Can I have your autograph?' You feel like saying to them 'Look, this is not why I got into this, and I don't really give a flying fuck whether you have my autograph or not and I'd rather you didn't bother me because if I was anyone else in the street you wouldn't.'**
THOM YORKE, RADIOHEAD

I think every citizen's got a right to mouth off – but it seems when I mouth off, I'm labelled pretentious.
**JEAN JACQUES BURNEL. THE STRANGLERS**

**I'm beginning to think that it's easier to scare people than to make them laugh.** JIM MORRISON, THE DOORS

I get tired of singing to the guys I beat up in motion pictures. **ELVIS PRESLEY**

**What I have to fall back on is my own isolated existence.** BOB DYLAN

The thing that more than anything annoys me about the paparazzi is that they really feel they have put you where you are. They really think that because you're a celebrity you owe them all the pictures they can get. I think it's completely unfair. **MADONNA**

**When Joan (Baez) and I sing 'Blowing In The Wind', it's like an old folk song to me. It never occurs to me that I'm the person who wrote that.** BOB DYLAN

" You know, songs often have a very coloured past. They might have something about them but it still doesn't work, so someone else adds a bit, and someone else adds a bit so perhaps one day I'll know its full history. "
**KYLIE MINOGUE**

" You won't get 'I love you baby' or 'suck my wee wee' from me; I try to write interesting lyrics. "
JELLO BIAFRA, DEAD KENNEDYS

## " MY PERSONA IS SO CONFUSED IT EVEN CONFUSES ME. " DAVID BOWIE

" A game is closed field, a ring of death with sex at the centre. Performing is the only game I've got. "
JIM MORRISON, THE DOORS

" Basically, our situation is on the borderline of collapse all the time anyway. " **JERRY GARCIA, THE GRATEFUL DEAD**

" I don't want to be a clown any more. I don't want to be a rock'n'roll star. " JIMI HENDRIX

" I refuse to slap some stupid words on the stupid paper just so we have a stupid song finished. " **SUZANNE VEGA**

" You tumble into that depression... there's nothing else for it, so you write your way out of it really, and that's when you really start looking at your life and trying to write about it. " JOHNNY BORRELL, RAZORLIGHT

" Music is a lot of hard work; it is not something you leave at the office. This is a twenty-four hour a day job. I've been criticised and maligned and misunderstood. This is something I take around with me all the time. "
**DON HENLEY, THE EAGLES**

**A person doing experimental music must be responsible for the results of his experiments. They could be very dangerous, emotionally.** FLORIAN SCHNEIDER, KRAFTWERK

Altamont, it could only happen to the Stones. Let's face it. It wouldn't happen to The Bee Gees and it wouldn't happen to Crosby, Stills & Nash. **KEITH RICHARDS**

**Probably, the biggest bringdown of my life was being in a pop group and finding out how much it was like everything it was supposed to be against.**

MAMA CASS ELLIOT, THE MAMAS & THE PAPAS

If you were a normal person walking down the street, they wouldn't come up to you and say 'cor, I think you're ugly'. If you're famous, they think it's a right. **GARY NUMAN**

**People have the wrong idea about us. They think we're a bunch of trans-sexual junkies or something.**

ARTHUR KANE, NEW YORK DOLLS

# "I'M A FREAKIN' ARTIST, MAN, NOT A FUCKING RACEHORSE." JOHN LENNON

**I'm just gonna keep on rocking', 'cos if I start saving up bits and pieces of me like that, man, there ain't gonna be nothing left for Janis.** JANIS JOPLIN

One has to completely humiliate oneself to be what The Beatles were, and that's what I resent. **JOHN LENNON**

**People take us far too seriously. We're going to have to start being far more stupid.** DAVID BYRNE, TALKING HEADS

Do you want an exclusive? Today, I trod on a spider. And yesterday, a rabbit died only seven and a half miles from my home. Didn't you know I'm the bad boy of the group? I say words like 'bum'. **LES McKEOWN, BAY CITY ROLLERS**

**I should be more understood. It doesn't matter that I carry a gun, or have bodyguards, or live in a fortified mansion. When I go into a recording studio, I make Art.** PHIL SPECTOR

There is a bad image about electronic music. In the minds of many people it means... vacuum cleaners. **JEAN-MICHEL JARRE**

**Most everybody had written me off. Oh yeah, they all acted like they were proud for me when I straightened up. Some of them are still mad about it, though. I didn't go ahead and die so that they'd have a legend to sing about and put me in hillbilly heaven.** JOHNNY CASH

Writers can say what they like about me. That I'm skinny, that I'm ugly, that I got pimples. I don't care. The only thing that disturbs me is when someone questions my integrity. **PATTI SMITH**

**I didn't leave the band, the band left me. No comment on the reasons why... it stopped the rise of 'The Rolling Stones of the 1980s' ever happening.** JOHNNY ROTTEN

One night, nobody was paying any attention to me, so I thought I'd commit suicide. So I went in the bathroom, broke a glass and slashed my chest with it. It's a really good way to get attention. I'm going to do it again, particularly as it doesn't work. **SID VICIOUS**

PINK

**❝I was very lonely, actually. When I was eight, I tried to commit suicide to get noticed by my parents. I used to do things like fall on the floor upstairs so they'd think I'd fallen downstairs. And I'd always have bottles of pills in my hands. I've always felt on the outside. ❞** SIOUXSIE SIOUX

❝You can't be creative when you're completely happy. ❞ **PINK**

**❝The boy has his vision, but it was time for me, as an adult, to have another dream. I realised I didn't have any ambition. ❞** VAN MORRISON

❝I get into one of those dark, melancholy moods and I just milk it for everything I can. ❞ **LOU REED**

**❝I don't think I'm very intelligent. My IQ has dropped in the last year. I don't know, I think it's terrible. I can't speak to people properly any more. I think it's because I don't read so much any more. Reading does a lot for your brain. ❞** PAUL WELLER, THE JAM

❝To me, the nut of the thing is that if what you make is hard like a diamond, you can put it anywhere. You can put it up your ass and it will still be beautiful ❞ **IGGY POP**

**❝I'm only twenty-two and I feel I've seen everything. It makes it very difficult sometimes. ❞** JOHN LYDON

❝If I read anything cruel, I have to have a couple of days to get over it. If it came at me all the time, I'd go around throwing acid into people's faces. ❞ **DEBBIE HARRY, BLONDIE**

" Sometimes I can make myself feel better with music, but other times it's still hard to go to sleep at night. "
BOB DYLAN

" I love talking about the various ways in which I am unappreciated. " LEONARD COHEN

" I feel I'm a catalyst for the movement, but my personal life is shot. " JOHNNY ROTTEN

" I changed my hairstyle so many times now I don't know what I look like. " DAVID BYRNE, TALKING HEADS

" When I was about twelve, I used to think I must be a genius, but nobody's noticed. I used to think either I'm a genius or I'm mad, which is it? I used to think, 'Well, I can't be mad because nobody's put me away; therefore, I'm a genius...' If there is such a thing as genius, I am one y'know... and if there isn't, I don't care. " JOHN LENNON

" I was too early for Star Wars, too late for 2001. "
DAVID BOWIE

" SOMEBODY TOLD ME THAT I DON'T MAKE SMALL-TALK AND THAT'S WHY MEN HATE ME. " YOKO ONO

" Sometimes we didn't know if we were playing great music or nonsense. It was a strange experience, flying around the world in a private plane and getting booze. An interesting way to make a living, but definitely strange. " ROBBIE ROBERTSON, THE BAND, ON BACKING DYLAN IN 1966

" I'm sick of being Gulliver... I just want to go home to Beckenham and watch the telly. "
DAVID BOWIE AFTER HIS 1974 TOUR

" If I wanted to get anything out of this business, it was never to have to go back and work in a factory again. But one thing I've learned is that money never buys you out of being working class. The middle classes never let you forget where you've come from. " ROGER DALTREY, THE WHO

**" Pleasure, I never seek pleasure. There was a time years ago when I sought a lot of pleasure because I'd had a lot of pain. But I found out there was a subtle relationship between pleasure and pain. So now I do what I have to do without looking for pleasure in it. "** BOB DYLAN

## " IT'S VERY HARD TO LIVE UP TO AN IMAGE. " ELVIS PRESLEY

**" Imagine taking off your make-up and nobody knows who you are. "** STEVEN TYLER, AEROSMITH

" In a way, it was like a sacrifice. We can do anything we want to now. I have very odd feelings. I feel incredibly strong and at the same time incredibly fragile. "
**ROGER DALTREY, ON KEITH MOON'S DEATH**

**" Encores for The New York Dolls was like having Christmas come round twice in one year. "**
SYLVAIN SYLVAIN, NEW YORK DOLLS

" Sometimes I wonder what all the fuss is about. We're the nicest bunch of guys you'd ever want to meet. "
**JOHNNY ROTTEN**

**" I can't feel strongly, I get too numb. "** DAVID BOWIE

" Along we go, we play through our LP tracks and we do our joke announcements and we do our commercial numbers and we do our movements. And then it comes to the end and we do 'My Generation' and we fucking smash everything up. **PETE TOWNSHEND, THE WHO, 1968**

**I'm not a genius. I'm just a hard-working guy.**
BRIAN WILSON

I know that one day, a big artist is going to be killed on stage... and I keep thinking, it's going to be me. **DAVID BOWIE**

DAVID BOWIE

**I was going on stage with a band that was a burn. It was like going out and selling parsley on the street and having to meet the people next day. Byrdshit! It wasn't The Byrds – it was the fucking canaries!** DAVID CROSBY

Fame threw me for a loop at first. I learned how to swim with it and turn it around. So you can just throw it in the closet and pick it up when you need it. **BOB DYLAN**

**I've been told I'm a genius. What do you think?**
PHIL SPECTOR

I'm interested in anything about revolt, disorder, chaos, especially activity that seems to have no meaning. **JIM MORRISON, THE DOORS**

**Success is like a shot of heroin. It's up to you do decide whether you want to continue to put the needle in your arm.** DON McLEAN

I have a terrible feeling that I'll wake up on my thirtieth birthday and my looks will have gone. **MARIANNE FAITHFULL**

**❝It's bloody difficult staying in bed for seven days when you are perfectly healthy.❞** JOHN LENNON

❝If I can't give people the best, I'd rather not appear at all.❞
**ELVIS PRESLEY**

**❝This country places a tremendous priority on being successful, but there is a tremendous lack of people who are good at what they do.❞** PAUL SIMON

PHIL SPECTOR

❝Have my best days gone? Truthfully, I have to answer 'yes'.❞
**PHIL SPECTOR**

**❝I believed it. I thought I was a fucking genius. Oh Christ, it ruined me.❞** KRIS KRISTOFFERSON

❝The most important thing in the world is to dig yourself, and if you can't do that, why in hell parade yourself around in front of an audience?❞ **DAVID JOHANSEN**

**❝When I get annoyed over something, I need an enemy – somebody who's done something to me - so I can take it out on them and beat them to a pulp.❞** SID VICIOUS

❝I don't think anybody ever made it with a girl because they had a Tom Waits album on their shelves. I've got all three, and it never helped me.❞ **TOM WAITS**

**❝ I'm always pissed off at something. It's the best position for observing. All these groups that get to the top get too content, then blow it with bad music. Our intention is to stay pissed off. ❞** TOM PETTY

# ❝ GODAMMIT! HE BEAT ME TO IT. ❞

**JANIS JOPLIN ON THE DEATH OF JIMI HENDRIX, 1970**

**❝ Sometimes I don't feel as if I'm a person at all. I'm just a collection of other people's ideas. ❞** DAVID BOWIE

❝ The only reason journalists call me a myth or a legend is because they simply can't think of anything else to write. ❞ **VAN MORRISON**

**❝ You can't rely on inspiration every night. ❞** JANIS JOPLIN

❝ If I had the capabilities of being something other than I am, I would. It's no fun being an artist. ❞ **JOHN LENNON**

**❝ If I don't talk to the press, I'm a hermit. If I talk to the press, I'm trying to manipulate. I can't win. ❞** BOB DYLAN

❝ I will never put anyone into the position of being humiliated. It happened to me for too long. ❞
**BRUCE SPRINGSTEEN**

**❝ Pain is what we're in most of the time. And I think the bigger the pain, the more Gods we need. ❞** JOHN LENNON

❝ I've been through it all. I've been the puppet, the arsehole, the dupe, the junkie and I've come through it and proved I'm the equal to anybody you'd care to mention. ❞ **IGGY POP**

**❝ I could never imagine a lot of people wanting this ugly geek in glasses ramming his songs down their throats. ❞** ELVIS COSTELLO

"QUITTING DRUGS IS LIKE HAVING SEX WITH A GORILLA, YOU'RE NOT DONE UNTIL THE GORILLA IS." MEGADETH

# CHAPTER EIGHT
# EXCESS ALL AREAS

> **Being fired from Hawkwind for drugs is a bit like being pushed off the Empire State Building for liking heights, you know? I was doing the wrong drugs. I was doing speed and they were all acid freaks. Mind you, I was doing acid as well, it was just one of those elitist numbers.** LEMMY, MOTÖRHEAD

> **Whoever said I'm on a line of cocaine every 40 minutes, I'll sue the fucker. That's out of order. Me and our Liam will take anything that's put in front of us because... that's just the kind of guys we are. But we've never been on stage out of it. We've never taken heroin or crack. We do take too many drugs, though...**
> **NOEL GALLAGHER, OASIS**

LEMMY

"I can honestly say, all the bad things that ever happened to me were directly, directly attributed to drugs and alcohol. I mean, I would never urinate at the Alamo at nine o'clock in the morning dressed in a woman's evening dress sober." OZZY OSBOURNE

"You sit and talk about your hopes and your band's music and they say, 'Yeah, that's great. We're really gonna cover your band.' Then you read **The Mirror** and it's like, '£1,000 a day on crack and heroin.' So the five minutes you spent talking about drugs is the article." **PETE DOHERTY**

"We've gone from on the farm smoking shitloads of hash and coming up with a load of mashed up tunes, to this time being more 'royal', should I say?" TOM MEIGHAN, KASABIAN

"I got straight and Aerosmith were still messing around with everything, you know the Toxic Twins? I showed up at one of their recording sessions, unannounced, and they were so screwed up that they told me later on they were so embarrassed to be so screwed up in front of Alice that the next day they decided to get straight!" **ALICE COOPER**

COURTNEY LOVE

"Reporting I'm drunk is like saying there was a Tuesday last week." GRACE SLICK, JEFFERSON AIRPLANE

**"** I would drink before I went on TV and somehow my shirt would come off. **"** COURTNEY LOVE

**"** I smoked fifty joints in the Sixties and snorted two lines of coke once in Detroit. It wasn't half as nice as a good lady, or a good meal for that matter. **"** TED NUGENT

**"** Forty-nine times with ad lib shouts of 'oh', 'oo', 'no', yells, moans, shrieks, groans, etc. **"**
CODA, SHEET MUSIC FOR 'COLD TURKEY' BY JOHN LENNON

## "I ONLY GET ILL WHEN I GIVE UP DRUGS." KEITH RICHARDS

**"** Each to their own but at the end of the day drugs are destructive, they'll destroy you. Drugs definitely played a part in the destruction of the Roses. We are all to blame. **"** IAN BROWN, STONE ROSES

**"** I'm sure we'd probably all be much happier and better party monsters if we indulged in Class A drugs, but we'd probably self-destruct six months down the line, which is what a lot of bands do. I'm not defending or condoning bands' use of drugs, it is a bizarre, precarious, insecure, paranoid, falsely-comfortable, perspective-distorting lifestyle. **"** COLIN GREENWOOD, RADIOHEAD

**"** I'm not a junkie and I won't even try it out. **"** NEIL YOUNG

**"** I love my country stuff. I just sing my pretty love songs and my drinking songs and leave it at that. **"**
JERRY LEE LEWIS

"With a person who is an alcoholic, as I am, you don't ever have one or two drinks. It doesn't work that way. I've never had two drinks in my life."
**GRACE SLICK, JEFFERSON AIRPLANE**

**"I feel sorry for the Nineties, because it was never able to be anything much more than the hangover to the party that was the Eighties."** SIMON LE BON, DURAN DURAN

"I don't take any stimulants or uppers. Every hour you stay up on coke or pills or whatever is an hour off the other end of your life. You see Errol Flynn when he was fifty? Jesus Christ! I'll be fifty in fifteen years and I'll be better looking that Flynn and I'll bet I can get it up quicker than he can. Whatever it and up is, I bet I can." IAN DURY

**"You know I love pot, and I love beer, but I am totally sober, just because it completely stopped working for me."** ANTHONY KIEDIS, RED HOT CHILI PEPPERS

"I was so into speed. I mean I don't even recall making the first album." **MICK JONES**

# "KNOWING ME, I'LL PROBABLY GET BUSTED AT MY OWN FUNERAL."
JIMI HENDRIX

"I spend all my money on drugs for other people. I want people to take drugs. It's better than playing Monopoly."
**LOU REED**

**"When Sid's out of it, he's a different person. At least if he goes to prison he'll kick his habit."**
STEVE JONES, ON FELLOW SEX PISTOL SID VICIOUS

**"** Everybody vomits now and then. **"** JOHNNY ROTTEN

**"** One time I bought a pound of grass and took four tablets of mescaline, a quarter of an ounce of cocaine and a bottle of tequila and I was out of my tree for a week. I had the worst fucking time of my entire life. I thought, 'That's it, I've done it now, I'm going to be here forever.' I was talking to horses – and the weird thing was they were talking back to me. **"** OZZY OSBOURNE

**"** I don't have a drink problem – except when I can't get one. **"** TOM WAITS

**"** I think drugs are purely a matter for the person concerned. It's like a blowjob – in some states that's still illegal. It's just a matter of how much people are prepared to put up with so-called authorities prying into their lives. **"**
KEITH RICHARDS

ALICE COOPER

**"** I sip. I don't drink a lot. I can go through four quiz shows on one beer. I use it as a prop anyhow. I don't drink to get drunk. I just drink out of habit now. **"**
**ALICE COOPER**

**I took two grams of biker speed, five trips of LSD, and as much grass as could be inhaled before the gig. I found this connection effective enough to completely lose my senses, and then before a gig we'd gather like a football team and hype ourselves up to a point, where we'd scream, 'OK guys, what're we gonna do? Kill! Kill! KILL!!. Then we'd take the stage.**

IGGY POP, ON THE STOOGES ERA

Les, the police are coming in through the windows.

**MICK JAGGER'S PHONE CALL TO PUBLICIST LES PERRIN DURING HIS 1969 BUST**

**Drugs are complete muck. Cocaine is the worst kind of drug ever.** MICK JONES, THE CLASH

I'm not into dope. That's true... I don't smoke grass and I don't like the things that everyone sniffs off a table. That's tawdry. It's so common. I like to play with my own system. Alone, I'm into drug masturbation. **LOU REED**

**Led Zeppelin's success may be attributable, at least in part, to the accelerating popularity of barbiturates and amphetamines – drugs that render their uses most responsive to crushing volume and ferocious histrionics.** LOS ANGELES TIMES

I only gave up drugs when the doctor told me I had six months to live. **KEITH RICHARDS**

**I used to sniff glue. It expanded my consciousness better than acid.** ACE FREHLEY, KISS

**"**I used to have to drink a fifth of tequila to sober up and do my shows. **"** **JERRY LEE LEWIS**

# **"I'VE SEEN THE BOTTOM OF A LOT OF BOTTLES."** CARL PERKINS

**"**You know, I'd really love to hear Frank Sinatra do 'Heroin'. Really. It would be just incredible to hear Frank Sinatra coming out with that song on some middle of the road radio station. Because that song doesn't mince words.**"** LOU REED

**"**I'm extremely careful. I've never turned blue in someone else's bathroom. I consider that the height of bad manners. I've had so many people do it to me and it's not really on, as far as drug etiquette goes, to turn blue in someone else's john. **"** **KEITH RICHARDS**

**"**Pills? I take pills all the time. I'll show you my briefcase – I'm a doctor. Aspirin, anything, I take it.**"**

RAY DAVIES, THE KINKS

LOU REED

"I DON'T OWN A GUN...
I OWN ABOUT 150 GUNS."

JAMES HETFIELD, METALLICA

# CHAPTER NINE
# OUT OF THEIR TREE

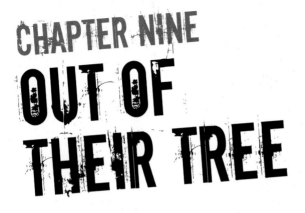

❝Rock music should be gross: that's the fun of it. It gets up and drops its trousers.❞ BRUCE DICKINSON, IRON MAIDEN

❝I listened to people effing and blinding during the Live Earth Concert last weekend and it just sounded so cheap. If you hear me swear on stage I'll give you all a tenner.❞
ROD STEWART

❝My goal in life is to give to the world what I was lucky to receive... the ecstasy of divine union through my music and my dance.❞ MICHAEL JACKSON

❝We are the Beavis and Butthead generation, whether we want to recognise it or not.❞
BILLY CORGAN, SMASHING PUMPKINS

❝I never used to dream about Jimi. But one night I had a dream and Jimi came into the room. I said, 'But you're dead' and he said, 'It's cool. I just wanted to see you again'.❞ NOEL REDDING, JIMI HENDRIX EXPERIENCE

❝We used to walk on stage to a reading of **Howl** by Allen Ginsburg. Not many bands did that in 1990. Not many bands do that now.❞ **NICKY WIRE, MANIC STREET PREACHERS**

**"Two weeks after Marc's death, I suddenly conceived. I've no idea why. Marc always had this thing about re-incarnation."** JUNE BOLAN, FORMER WIFE OF THE SINGER

**"**So I took out my hatchet and chopped the Holiday Inn room to bits. The television. The chairs. The cupboard doors. The bed. It happens all the time.**"**
**KEITH MOON, THE WHO**

**"I hate cleaning up lyrics for radio. I cringe every time I gotta fuckin' do it. But I got a choice. I could refuse to clean the shit up, meaning that it would never hit radio and I wouldn't have as big a voice in hip-hop as I wanna have. It's quite funny, though, singing 'chicken' instead of 'bitch'."** EMINEM

# "I LOVE BEETHOVEN, ESPECIALLY HIS POEMS." RINGO STARR

**"We wanted to see America. It wasn't entirely successful. I kept falling asleep, it was a long drive."**
MICK JONES, THE CLASH

**"**I got rabies shots for biting the head off a bat but that's OK – the bat had to get Ozzy shots.**"** OZZY OSBOURNE

**"If someone out there can gob into your mouth, well, it's the nearest thing you can get to a French kill at thirty yards."** PETE SHELLEY, BUZZCOCKS

**"**We're not ignored by the **Guinness Book Of Records**, but we've been largely ignored by the media during our lifetime. If you read any article, no mention is ever made of Pink Floyd. We're never included in the same sentences as The Beatles, The Rolling Stones and The Who.**"**
**ROGER WATERS, PINK FLOYD**

AMY WINEHOUSE

❝US crowds want explosions and naked women. But in the UK, you get cold women and warm beer, so there are downsides.❞

NICK VALENSI, THE STROKES

❝My lyrics are very personal and very intense, in a way. But I think there's a lot of humour in there as well. I've always wanted to present a point with a twist. You know, like 'I'm really angry about this, you're a bastard and you can't even get a boner!' I just want to say things I would find funny if I heard them.❞ **AMY WINEHOUSE**

❝People all over the world say, 'You're the guy who kills creatures? You still do it? You do it every night?' It happened fucking **once**, for Christ's sake.❞

OZZY OSBOURNE

❝You'd come offstage and still be buzzing. Then you'd go to a party and it would get out of hand. Things get broken. If you're sitting around after a show and there's things you don't like on telly, you just switch it off by throwing a bottle through the screen.❞ **KEITH MOON**

❝Listening to me and Kurt on You Tube last night we sound so young and dumb and cool. I wish I had been willing to do more with him but you didn't wanna get tarred with the Yoko brush.❞ COURTNEY LOVE

**"** All the equipment that I stole, that was the beginning of me being in music, that was it. That was the only way I knew how, to steal music equipment. And clothes. **"**
**STEVE JONES, THE SEX PISTOLS**

**" The weirdest thing is everybody actually thought I was trying to fit in but that I somehow got it wrong. Does it look like I'm trying to fit in with you? No. I didn't realise how sacred Hollywood is. It's like a religion, and I had a shit on the church floor. "**
BJORK ON WEARING HER 'SWAN' DRESS TO THE OSCARS

**"** Probably one word will always be akin to The Beach Boys, which is surfing. **"** **BRIAN WILSON**

**" People don't want to talk to you, y'know, if you're throwing up. Particularly if you're doing it in their room. If I throw up in my room, it's all right. "**
GRACE SLICK, JEFFERSON AIRPLANE

**"** Anybody that forms a group, writes songs and releases records and says they don't care if people like them are complete liars. **"**
**JAMES DEAN BRADFIELD, MANIC STREET PREACHERS**

**" I get my daughters to do it (downloading). I always looked on the computer as like, 'Well, now everybody wants to be a fucking typist.' "** KEITH RICHARDS

**"** I just don't hear anyone else making the music I'm making in my head, so I'll have to do it myself. **"** **BOB DYLAN**

**" It seems like the chaos of this world is accelerating, but so is the beauty in the consciousness of more and more people. "** ANTHONY KIEDIS, RED HOT CHILI PEPPERS

**"** You can tell by the kindness of a dog how a human should be. **"** **CAPTAIN BEEFHEART**

**"That's not my snake, you know. That snake was much larger than mine. I had to borrow it from a stripper in California when we played there. My snake had the 'flu and kept throwing up her mice."** ALICE COOPER

# "WE'RE THE McDONALDS OF ROCK. WE'RE ALWAYS THERE TO SATISFY, AND A BILLION SERVED." PAUL STANLEY, KISS

**"We're saying everything they want to say. The Dolls just reflect what's happening on the street, right? Truthfully, there's not too much to say about what's happening on the streets of New York and that's why The Dolls attract a lot of weirdos."** BILLY MURCIA, NEW YORK DOLLS

**"We can do what we couldn't do for nine years as The Beatles – we can go out shopping without being recognised."** GEORGE HARRISON, 1977

**"If you're a rock musician, you don't have to put on any airs and pretend to be all grown up."**
PETE TOWNSHEND, THE WHO

**"That's how I relax, with machines and things. I'm more at home playing with a telephone or digital clock or printing press than gardening or hanging out with people."**
IGGY POP

**"Why live in France? Because the French are so snobbish and into themselves that they don't even notice you."**
BONO

**"My teeth – I don't like the way they protrude. I'm going to have them done, but I haven't had the time. Apart from that, I'm perfect."** FREDDIE MERCURY, QUEEN

"THINK OF US AS EROTIC POLITICIANS."

JIM MORRISON, THE DOORS

# CHAPTER TEN
# WE ARE
# THE WORLD

**You have made people listen. You have made people care, and you have taught us that whether we are poor or prosperous, we have only one world to share. You have taught young people that they do have the power to change the world.**
KOFI ANNAN, UN SECRETARY GENERAL, ADDRESSING BONO,1999

Remember how much fun you had shooting spitwads at the teacher in seventh grade? Imagine applying that kind of attitude to actually fucking with Mitsubishi!
**JELLO BIAFRA, DEAD KENNEDYS**

**Politics? What a useless trip. If they're gonna drop the bomb, then drop it. But I don't want to write songs about it. Ecology? Man, I still throw coke bottles out of the window. Someone'll pick them up.** TOM PETTY

As a rock star, I have two instincts, I want to have fun, and I want to change the world. I have a chance to do both.
**BONO, U2**

**Politicians will fuck you up whoever they are. They never keep their promises.** LEMMY, MOTÖRHEAD

50 CENT

❝I think of The Beatles. They changed America, and not many people can say they changed America. And they did it with music. Not wars. Not laws. Not guns - none of that junk. They changed America with music and that's a pretty big deal.❞ **MARC ROBERGE, OAR**

❝**Nobody likes a stubborn, independent woman. I'm not shaking my ass to be famous.**❞ BONNIE RAITT

❝You wanna know something? I actually like George W. Bush. In some ways, I'm the George W. Bush of hip hop – nobody likes me, but I'm still gonna run it for the next four years.❞ **50 CENT**

❝**Subversive? Of course we're subversive. But if they really believe that you can start a revolution with a record, they're wrong. I wish we could. We're more subversive at live appearances.**❞ KEITH RICHARDS

❝Feminism has become a dirty word. Girl Power is just a Nineties way of saying it. We can give feminism a kick up the arse. Women can be so powerful when they show solidarity.❞ **SPICE GIRLS**

❝**You can't change the world with rock'n'roll, but if you can change it with anything at all, it's worth trying.**❞ TOM ROBINSON

**"**I'm not going to be fucked around by men in suits sitting on their fat arses in the city.**"**
**JOHN LENNON, DURING THE BEATLES' BREAK-UP**

**"If you believe in a cause, you must be willing to put yourself on the line for that cause."**
ADAM CLAYTON, U2, IN WAR-TORN BOSNIA

**"**I laugh at them. I laugh at those parlour-pink revolutionary kids going around saying 'I am a revolutionary by trade'. Bull fucking pukie – they haven't any idea what it is, man.**"** **DAVID CROSBY**

# "I ALWAYS THOUGHT THE ARISTOCRACY SHOULD BE SHOT. I WAS BROUGHT UP THAT WAY." IAN BROWN, STONE ROSES

**"**People don't need us to tell them how messed up the world is, but that's what we're doing. The difference is that because I have faith and hope and am interested in love, it's my way of walking through the world. But I think you've got to see it and stare at those devils. The way is not to turn your face from them. U2 is painting a picture of a bleak landscape but somehow there is some kind of sunlight there.**"** **BONO, U2**

**"I've often said that rock is far higher than politics, and I know it sounds a bit pompous but I still believe that. The feeling that happens when you're listening to a really great piece of rock music or that you feel at a really great concert is much higher than anything you'll get at a political rally."** PETE TOWNSHEND, THE WHO

" From politicians, we get the sense, whether it's deserved or not - usually it is - we get the sense that everything they do is packaged and artificial and calculated and for their own benefit. " **JOHN LEGEND**

" **I vote for the weirdo, I vote for the loonies, I vote for the people off the left wall, I vote for the individuals.** "
JOE STRUMMER

" We're ashamed the president of the United States is from Texas. " **NATALIE MAINES, DIXIE CHICKS**

# "I'M SURPRISED WE AREN'T ALL IN JAIL FOR TREASON."

JOHNNY ROTTEN, AFTER 'GOD SAVE THE QUEEN'

" I think [rock] has [changed the world]. To me, it speaks of freedom of thought and individualism. And when we're all thinking, we can save the world. So in some ways, I think rock can save the world and in other ways, I think it already has. " **PAUL McCARTNEY**

" **I think the administration took September 11 and used it as a blank cheque. And like most Americans, I'm not sure the case has been made to put our sons and our daughters and innocent citizens at risk at this particular moment. But I don't think that's gonna matter, unfortunately.** " BRUCE SPRINGSTEEN

" I can relate to farmers in the Depression getting together in unions better that I could relate to you if you want to go to San Francisco and put a flower in your hair. "
**ROBBIE ROBERTSON, THE BAND**

**❝You have proven something to the world – that half a million kids can get together for fun and music and have nothing but fun and music.❞**
MAX YASGUR, OWNER OF THE WOODSTOCK FESTIVAL GROUNDS

**❝'It can't happen here' is number one on the list of famous last words.❞** DAVID CROSBY

BONO

The world is more malleable than you think and it's waiting for you to hammer it into shape.❞ **BONO, U2**

**❝I know nothing about politics. It doesn't mean much who's in power anyway, does it? This country's so bland it could be Hitler and no-one would notice, except of course, those self-righteous SWP people who I really loathe. Those hardline lefties have always hated rock music.❞** JOHN LYDON, PIL

**❝**I don't profess to be the messiah of slum people, but I was a back street kid and that hot little demon is still there, shovelling the hot coal in.❞ **OZZY OSBOURNE, BLACK SABBATH**

**❝The 1967 bust kind of said, 'from now on it's heavy'. Up till then it had been showbiz. Then you knew they considered you outside. They decide who lives outside the law. You're just living.❞** KEITH RICHARDS

**❝**The Devil always comes in between politicians and they start quarrelling. Y'have to imagine what really go on, because power become a pride business instead of we live together and trade together and stop the war.❞
**BOB MARLEY**

**“**This is our moment, this is our time, this is our chance to stand up for what is right. Three thousand Africans, mostly children, die every day of mosquito bites. We can fix that. Nine thousand people dying every die of a preventable, treatable disease like Aids. We have got the drugs. We can help them.**”** BONO

**“**If this world has a revolution, I know I'll really enjoy myself.**”** TOYAH WILLCOX

**“**It's not politics – just the difference between right and wrong.**”** PAUL SIMONON, THE CLASH

DAVID BOWIE

**“**I've seen life and I think I know who's controlling the world. And after what I've seen of the state of this world. I've never been so damned scared in all my life.**”**

**DAVID BOWIE**

**“**In 1967 we thought we'd stop the Vietnam war in about two years and instead it probably took us six or eight years, but I think everybody felt that this was the first time that the American people had actually forced the American government to be responsible to us and to stop doing something that they very much wanted to keep doing.**”** DAVID CROSBY

**"** You can't trust politicians. It doesn't matter to me who makes a political speech. It's all lies... and it applies to any rock star who wants to make a political speech as well. **"** BOB GELDOF

**"** We have fun, the kids have fun, the cops have fun. It's kind of a weird triangle. **"** JIM MORRISON, THE DOORS

# **" WE'RE TIRED OF JERKING OFF - WE WANT TO START FUCKING AGAIN. "**
JERRY GARCIA, GRATEFUL DEAD

**"** I've always been attracted to ideas that were about revolt against authority. When you make your peace with authority you become authority. **"** JIM MORRISON, THE DOORS

**"** We have been trained to be impotent. **"** JOAN BAEZ

**"** We've got absolutely nothing to do with any political party. We don't lean left or right, don't give a fuck about any of it... we don't believe in anarchy. It's fairly obvious that it doesn't work. It's a noble idea, but it's like suppressing human emotion. **"** PAUL WELLER, THE JAM

**"** Either you think you can change the system from within or you think the system is so corrupt you need a new system. I tend to favour the latter. **"** JARVIS COCKER

**"** It's power that runs this country. You can't change things overnight with a hit single. Rock singers getting into politics is rather stupid. **"** ELTON JOHN

**"** I think that people should go into public office for a term or two and then get back into their businesses and live under the laws that they passed. **"**
MIKE CURB, PRESIDENT OF WARNER/CURB RECORDS

❝ We were discriminated against all the time. If we were coloured, we'd really be able to kick up a stink about it. I'm not, so I have to put up with it. Everyone with long hair does. ❞ JIMMY PAGE

❝ It's a bit difficult to get hippies organised into anything. ❞
**GRACE SLICK, JEFFERSON AIRPLANE**

❝ **THE LESS YOU KNOW, THE MORE YOU BELIEVE.** ❞ BONO

❝ The BBC is a great quivering mess creeping into the 1940s out of the 1920s. ❞ **JOHN PEEL, 1967**

❝ **You smash it – I'll build around it.** ❞ JOHN LENNON

❝ Bands who crusade for causes are necessarily being hypocritical. They are always as interested in hits as in causes. One hand is raised in a power salute while the other is backhanding for cash. You can't sell revolutions. ❞ **BOB GELDOF**

❝ **It's a bit patronising for us 21 year olds to try to start to change the world. Especially when we're using enough power for 10 houses just for (stage) lighting. It'd be a bit hypocritical.** ❞ MATT HELDERS, ARCTIC MONKEYS

❝ The actual war against terrorism is extremely complicated. You try not to be cynical, but without the distraction of Iraq, (people would notice) that the economy is doing poorly, and the old-fashioned Republican tax cuts for the folks that are doing well will seriously curtail services for people who are struggling out there. I don't think that's the kind of country that Americans really want. ❞ **BRUCE SPRINGSTEEN**

**❝ I don't understand why people are talking about The Clash being a political band. I didn't know who the Prime Minister was until a couple of weeks ago. ❞**

PAUL SIMONON

**❝** 'Protest' is not my word. I've never thought of myself as such. The word 'protest', I think, was made up for people undergoing surgery... a normal person in his righteous mind would have to have hiccups to pronounce it properly. **❞** BOB DYLAN

BOB DYLAN

**❝ I'm gong to run for President and when I get elected I'll assassinate myself – that'll set a precedent. ❞**

SPENCER DRYDEN, JEFFERSON AIRPLANE

**❝** I've always felt alienated from the Woodstock Generation, felt out of psychedelia, because like most pop musicians I was into it before the masses and when it became big, I was extremely ill. **❞** PETE TOWNSHEND, THE WHO

**❝ The Indian's never going to get a damn thing till he goes out and scalps a few people. Then he'll get attention ❞**

RAY CHARLES

"I WOULD RATHER HAVE A CUP OF TEA THAN SEX." BOY GEORGE

# CHAPTER ELEVEN
# ALL YOU NEED IS LOVE?

> **For boys of our age it was a dream come true: girls on tap. It was crazy. We were just a bunch of lads let loose in the sweet shop. There was always some girl who'd come up and say 'Take me back with you'. I wouldn't even spend the night with them, I wanted a good night's sleep. You'd get them back to your room, do the business and then say, 'Right, out'. It's amazing how desensitised you become if it's continuous.** GARY BARLOW, TAKE THAT

> The only things I was ever in love with were a mirror and a beer mug. **SID VICIOUS**

> **I do want people to know the songs that I wrote when I was with women were really about women, and the songs I have written since have been fairly obviously about men.** GEORGE MICHAEL

> Awww, I just wanted to see what it looked like in the spotlight. That's all.
> **JIM MORRISON, THE DOORS, ON EXPOSING HIMSELF ON STAGE**

> **Instead of getting married again, I'm going to find a woman I don't like and just give her a house.**
> ROD STEWART

❝How can you consider flower power outdated? The essence of my lyrics is the desire for peace and harmony. That's all anyone has ever wanted. How could it become outdated?❞ **ROBERT PLANT, LED ZEPPELIN**

❝**The more successful I become, the more I need a man.**
BEYONCE

❝I thought everybody in rock had illegitimate children.❞
**ROD STEWART**

❝**It wasn't Trent (Reznor, it was) his guitarist came onstage, pulled down his pants and was trying to embarrass us. I grabbed him and put his dick in my mouth and sent him on his way. So it wasn't really a full-scale blowjob, I don't even think his dick was hard so I don't know whether that counts. But my parents were in the audience and they didn't mind so I don't know why anyone else should. Sex is so basic. It's all rock'n'roll to me.❞** MARILYN MANSON

❝I'm very, very 'country music' in my attitude to talking about my marriage.❞ **ELVIS COSTELLO**

❝**I wanted to be an actress and a scholar, too. My first move was to get a Rolling Stone as a boyfriend. I slept with three then decided that the singer was the best bet.❞** MARIANNE FAITHFULL

**"** There is nothing wrong with going to bed with someone of your own sex. People should be very free with sex, they should draw the line at goats. **"** ELTON JOHN

**" Fuck Grace Slick? I never even kissed her. And it's the smartest, best thing I ever done. "** MARTY BALIN

**"** An awful lot of gay pop stars pretend to be straight. I'm going to start a movement of straight pop stars pretending to be gay. **"** ROBBIE WILLIAMS

**" I WISH I COULD HANG WITH DYKES, BUT I'VE GOT COCK WRITTEN ALL OVER MY BROW. "** COURTNEY LOVE

**"** Why can't you share your bed? The most loving thing to do is to share your bed with someone. It's very charming. It's very sweet. It's what the whole world should do. **"**
MICHAEL JACKSON

**" It was like a fish discovering water for the first time. I just swam from there on. "** TOM ROBINSON, ON HIS 'COMING OUT'

**"** A symbol of the scarlet woman, that was my claim to fame. **"** MARIANNE FAITHFULL

**" I think I mentioned to Bob [Geldof] I could make love for eight hours. What I didn't say was that this included four hours of begging and then dinner and a movie. "** STING

**"** When I was thirteen, all I desperately wanted to do was have sex. I did it with boys at school. I think that's true of almost every boy. **"** MICK JAGGER

**It wasn't a real wedding. We were getting married to get loads of money for it. I was too young to understand what having kids meant. Having a child was like getting a dog.** BRIAN McFADDEN, EX-WESTLIFE, ON MARRIAGE TO EX-ATOMIC KITTEN KERRY KATONA

I can't believe Brian could be so callous and cruel. Our children were born out of love. For him to compare having children to getting a dog is just cruel and downright evil. **KERRY KATONA**

**I think what you have to realise is that our generation is the first generation since its sexual awakening has come into the world and realised that sex can mean, ultimately, death.** BRIAN MOLKO, PLACEBO

## "LOVE IS TWO MINUTES AND 52 SECONDS OF SQUELCHING NOISES."
**JOHNNY ROTTEN**

**I just don't like to get intimate. I don't want anyone to know what I feel and think, and if they can't get an idea of what sort of person I am through my music then that's too bad.** KURT COBAIN, NIRVANA

You may as well learn about sex from Motley Crue than your parents – it's a lot more fun. **NIKKI SIXX, MÖTLEY CRÜE**

**The Sun in London ran a front page declaring my bum a national treasure. I really did laugh at that. It's not like it can actually do anything, except wiggle.** KYLIE MINOGUE

As far as I'm concerned, the benefit of being a black Irishman is that I pull more chicks. **PHIL LYNOTT, THIN LIZZY**

> **If I'm in the middle of hitting a most fantastic cross court back hand top spin and someone says 'Can you stop now and have sex' I'll say: 'No thanks!'** CLIFF RICHARD

> I do have the chromosomes of a gay man. It's intrinsic.
> **ANA MATRONIC, SCISSOR SISTERS**

> **Sometimes an orgasm is better than being on stage. Sometimes being on stage is better than an orgasm.**
> MICK JAGGER

> Faggot to me doesn't necessarily mean gay person. Faggot to me means pussy, cissy, if you're a man, be a man, know what I'm saying, that's the worse thing you can say to a man, it's like callin' 'em a girl, whether he's gay or not. Growing up, me and my friends, faggot was a word, like 'You're bein' a fuckin' fag, man, you're bein' a fag', nobody really thought gay person, I never thought, 'You're bein' a gay person.' **EMINEM**

EMINEM

> **I didn't like fucking then, and I still don't. It's dull.**
> SID VICIOUS

> It was an excessive time, from every possible point of view. I was never particularly great with girls at school, so when the band took off I just went crazy. I really did shag myself senseless. **SIMON LE BON, DURAN DURAN**

**Any bright girl would understand that if I were gay, I'd say the same things about guys.**

MICK JAGGER, REFUTING CHARGES OF SEXIST LYRICS

**Sometimes, I feel I'm losing interest in sex entirely.**

**MICK JONES, THE CLASH**

**We're all kinky – we're just admitting that we're sick.**

NIKKI SIXX, MÖTLEY CRÜE

**The concentration on my sexuality is the result of my own honesty. It's my own fault. By talking.**

**DEBBIE HARRY, BLONDIE**

**You can't just go to bed with a cup of hot chocolate.**

JOHN BONHAM, LED ZEPPELIN

**I am the only man who can say he's been in Take That and at least two members of the Spice Girls.** **ROBBIE WILLIAMS**

**I only remember a city by its chicks.** JIMI HENDRIX

**You don't go grabbin' somebody's husband's balls, you understand me? That's very disrespectful.**

**FAITH HILL TO A FAN OF HER HUSBAND, TIM McGRAW**

**What's the big deal? I have really strong morals, and just because I look sexy on the cover of Rolling Stone doesn't mean I'm a naughty girl. I'd do it again. I thought the pictures were fine. And I was tired of being compared to Debbie Gibson and all of this bubblegum pop all the time.** BRITNEY SPEARS

“You know, The Beatles' tours were like Fellini's **Satyricon**. I mean, we had that image, but man, our tours were like something else. When we hit town, we hit it. We were not pissing around.” JOHN LENNON

“Love is what you feel for a dog or a pussycat, it doesn't apply to humans and if it does it just shows how low you are. It shows your intelligence isn't clicking.” JOHNNY ROTTEN, SEX PISTOLS

“Domesticity is death.” MICK JAGGER

“MAYBE THESE GIRLS WANT TO SLEEP WITH ME BECAUSE I SING QUITE WELL.” MICK HUCKNALL, SIMPLY RED

“Aids is like the Black Death isn't? But Aids isn't going to stop anybody doing anything. There's always something to stop you enjoying yourself isn't there? Getting laid is part of rock, and I'd sooner get laid than have to give it up.” LEMMY, MOTÖRHEAD

“Self-denial is a great thing.” GILBERT O'SULLIVAN

“I'm choosy; I was a virgin until I was twenty.” GREGG ALLMAN

“You are all a bunch of fucking idiots. Your faces are pressed into the shit of the world. Take your fucking friend and love him. Do you want to see my cock?” JIM MORRISON, THE DOORS, SHORTLY PRIOR TO EXPOSING HIMSELF ON STAGE

“I don't want to see any faces at this party I haven't sat on.” BONNIE RAITT

**He sure left his mark, that cat. I know of five kids, at least, all by different chicks and they all look like Brian.** KEITH RICHARDS ON BRIAN JONES

I don't give a shit about gay, if they wanna be then that's their fuckin' business. Don't try that shit on me, don't come around me with that shit but, hey, as long as they ain't hurtin' nobody, ain't hurtin' me, whatever, be gay, do your thing, if you take it in the ass, you take it in the ass, you suck dick, whatever, that's your business. **EMINEM**

**I'm pretty much over my affection for men. The only time I get halfway wistful for those old days is in Japan. All those little boys are so cute I just want to take them all up to my room.** DAVID BOWIE

# "I DIVED INTO THE CROWD AND THE FIRST THING SOME GUY DID WAS GRAB MY TITS". **COURTNEY LOVE**

**I think that women have got it made if they know how to go about it. A woman don't have to work, really, if she don't want to and is smart enough to make a man a good wife, he's gonna take care of her.** DOLLY PARTON

We steer completely clear of anything suggestive. We take a lot of care with lyrics because we don't want to offend anybody. The music is the main thing and it's just as easy to write acceptable words. **BILL HALEY, 1954**

**I keep saying I wish I had as much in bed as I get in the newspapers. Then I'd be real busy.** LINDA RONSTADT

I'm sexy. How can I avoid it? That's the essence of me. I would have to put a bag over my head and body but then

my voice would come across. And it's sexy. "
**MADONNA**

MADONNA

" Birds are all right. They're all pink on the inside. Any bird who's fit is all right, unless she's nicked or ugly and she speaks backwards to you. If she thinks I'm boss, then thumbs up. Chicks in Japan don't even ask you your name, just 'Can I sleep with you tonight?' Certainly, my dear. I like American birds till they open their mouths. Then they annoy me. But if they're fit, they're fit. " LIAM GALLAGHER, OASIS

" Intellectually, of course, we didn't believe in getting married. But one doesn't love someone intellectually. "
**JOHN LENNON**

" There's really no reason to have women on a tour unless they've got a job to do. The only other reason is to screw. Otherwise they'd get bored. They just sit around and moan. " MICK JAGGER

" Mick had me on a pin and he couldn't let me go. He had me on a pin and he was watching me fail and writhe, but it was something that fascinated him as an artist. "
**MARIANNE FAITHFULL, ON MICK JAGGER**

" On stage, I make love to 25,000 different people, then I go home alone " JANIS JOPLIN

YOKO ONO

" When we started filming, I could feel George looking at me and I was a bit embarrassed. Then, when he was giving me his autograph, he put seven kisses under his name. I thought he must like me a little. "

**PATTI HARRISON, NEE BOYD, ON MEETING HER FUTURE HUSBAND WHILE PLAYING A SCHOOLGIRL IN A HARD DAY'S NIGHT**

**" Men have an unusual talent for making a bore out of everything they touch. "** YOKO ONO

" Over here they put girls into two categories – either you're a sweet, clean-cut girl, or a real nasty bitch. And I know which they've figured me out to be. " **DEBBIE HARRY, BLONDIE**

**" You can't blame John for falling in love with Yoko any more than you can blame me for falling in love with Linda. At the beginning I was annoyed with him, jealous because of Yoko and afraid about the break-up of a great musical partnership. It took me a year to realise they were in love. "** PAUL McCARTNEY

" People equate sexy with promiscuous. They think that because I'm shaped this way, I must be scandalous – like running around and bringing men into my hotel room. But it's just the opposite. " **JENNIFER LOPEZ**

**" A lot of tunes in the guise of romanticism have mainly fucking behind them. "** RANDY NEWMAN

" People are really surprised when they meet us and find out that we're all straight. " **ALICE COOPER**

**I had a rough time in school because I was the most popular girl in the wrong way... I had a lot of stories told on me, a lot of lies, just because I looked the way I did. I was always big in the boobs, small in the waist and big in the butt. I just grew up that way, and I had that foxy personality too.** DOLLY PARTON

I've lived for years with people saying I'm a poof but I don't give a damn. My best friends know me and that's all that matters. Even before I became a Christian, I wasn't going to lay loads of chicks to prove myself. I'm about the only one around who hasn't had a nervous breakdown.
CLIFF RICHARD

**I think pop music has done more for oral intercourse than anything else that ever happened, and vice versa.** FRANK ZAPPA

Being gay wasn't a prerequisite for everyone joining the band. I wanted good musicians. I mean – Joni Mitchell presumably doesn't grill people who apply for a job in her band, saying 'Are you a woman?' TOM ROBINSON

**I think I'm more grounded, you know, and I know what I want out of life and I'm, you know, my morals are really, you know, strong and I have major beliefs about certain things and I think that has helped me, you know, from being, you know, coming from a really small town.**
BRITNEY SPEARS

The great thing about being thirty is that there are a great deal more available women. The young ones look younger and the old ones don't look nearly as old.
**GLENN FREY, THE EAGLES**

**❝I love to hear boys shouting for me, just like I shouted for the Stones.❞** PATTI SMITH

❝Everybody is either heterosexual or homosexual in London, but no-one ever gets laid.❞
**DAVID JOHANSEN, NEW YORK DOLLS**

**❝I've never brought that open marriage thing. I've never seen it work. But that doesn't mean I believe in monogamy. Sleeping with someone else doesn't necessarily constitute an infidelity... What does is having sex with someone and telling your spouse... anything you feel guilty about.❞** CARLY SIMON

❝Sex is about as important as a cheese sandwich. But a cheese sandwich, if you ain't got one to put in your belly, is extremely important.❞ **IAN DURY**

**❝Maybe if the audience can see a cock through a pair of trousers, that must make you a sex symbol.❞**
ROBERT PLANT, LED ZEPPELIN

❝You look for certain things in certain towns. Chicago, for instance, is notorious for sort of two things at once. Balling two chicks, or three, in combination acts.❞
**JIMMY PAGE, LED ZEPPELIN**

**❝Uh-oh, I think I exposed myself out there.❞**
JIM MORRISON, THE DOORS

❝Marriage is worse than dying. Why stay with one person for fifty years. We advise against marriage.❞ **JOEY RAMONE**

**❝The Bay City Rollers aren't wholesome, they're just particular about whom they sleep with.❞**
TAM PATON, MANAGER OF THE BAND

**"** It's really maddening to us as women to see young girls just lay themselves at the feet of any male who happens to be involved with rock'n'roll. It's a really sad sight, like sheep to the slaughter. **"** ANN WILSON, HEART

**"** You know how Americans are – when it comes to sex, the men can't keep from lying and the women can't keep from telling the truth. **"**
ROBIN ZANDER, CHEAP TRICK, ON BEING VOTED 1977'S SEXIEST MAN BY A NEW JERSEY WOMEN'S CLUB

# "GIVE ME A COUPLE OF DRINKS, AND I'LL BE THE BITCH." " ELTON JOHN

**"** We thought it was modern to have a female in the group who wasn't featuring her voice and breasts. **"**
CHRIS FRANTZ, ON TALKING HEADS' TINA WEYMOUTH

**"** Rock'n'roll meant fucking, originally. That's what it originally meant, which I don't think is a bad idea. Let's bring it back again. **"** WAYLON JENNINGS

**"** You were at school and you were pimply and no-one wanted to know you. You get into a group and you've got thousands of chicks there. And there you are with thousands of little girls screaming their heads off. Man it's power... phew! **"** ERIC CLAPTON

**"** I just know that if I got mixed up in a love affair, then it would affect my work. It would ruin everything for me. That's why I'm denying myself. **"** GILBERT O'SULLIVAN

"I DON'T LISTEN TO MUSIC, I HATE ALL MUSIC"

JOHNNY ROTTEN

# CHAPTER TWELVE
# THE RULES OF ROCK

**❝I don't know anything about music. In my line you don't have to.❞** ELVIS PRESLEY

**❝**We're a very expensive group; we break a lot of rules. It's unheard of to combine opera with a rock theme, my dear.**❞ FREDDIE MERCURY, QUEEN**

**❝I always thought the good thing about the guitar was that they didn't teach it in school.❞** JIMMY PAGE, LED ZEPPELIN

**❝**Actually '78 was a really exciting time for U2. We had just discovered F sharp minor. So we had the fourth chord and we'd only had three up to then.**❞ BONO, U2**

**❝I usually like to make really dramatic songs [that are] dynamic from part to part – a lot of jumping from really quiet to really loud.❞** MC MIKE SHINODA, LINKIN PARK

**❝**There are countries where the organizers don't know what they're doing or what's going on – but I wouldn't name Italy and Spain!**❞ ROBERT SMITH, THE CURE**

**❝It's not the size of the ship, it's the size of the waves.❞**
LITTLE RICHARD

❝I'm the first to admit I'm no virtuoso. I can't play like Segovia. The flip side of that is that Segovia could probably never have played like me. ❞ **KURT COBAIN, NIRVANA**

❝**I accept chaos, I wonder if it accepts me.**❞ BOB DYLAN

❝The down side of being outrageous is that you have to go around explaining your fucking self to people. If you're too cocky, somebody might just pull out a fucking gun and cock it and blow your fucking face off. You gotta be really careful what you bite off. Don't bite off more than you can chew. It's a dangerous world. ❞ **OZZY OSBOURNE**

❝**We're doing it girls, so can you. Even if you have to shout a bit louder, barge through all these people, then do it!**❞ EMMA BUNTON, SPICE GIRLS

❝Turn the other cheek too often and you get a razor through it. ❞ **JOHNNY ROTTEN**

❝**I only got seventh-grade education, but I have a doctorate in funk, and I like to put that to good use.**❞ JAMES BROWN

❝I'm just as sick as the others, although I prefer to do my sickness in private. ❞ **MICK MARS, MÖTLEY CRÜE**

❝**I hardly ever listen to any of our old stuff now. Once the songs have been recorded and put on to vinyl they become someone else's entertainment, not mine.**❞ ROBERT SMITH, THE CURE

❝Everyone admires the poet, no matter if he's a lumberjack, a football player or a car thief. If he's a poet, he'll be admired and respected. ❞ **BOB DYLAN**

**" As the song says, 'Rock'n'roll is my religion and my law.' I believe in rock'n'roll. I can feel rock'n'roll. I'm involved in rock'n'roll. I get a great kick out of playing rock'n'roll and the kick I get is out of seeing all those people with happy smiles on their faces. "** OZZY OSBOURNE

**"** Music is one family, but the word is the thing. Words can teach children something. It is something really serious, not entertainment. You entertain people who are satisfied. Hungry people cannot be entertained, or people who are afraid. You can't entertain a man who has no food. **"**
**BOB MARLEY**

**" We've been getting in touch with our feminine sides – we've been touching them every day – and we've been beating our inner child. "**
JOSH HOMME, QUEENS OF THE STONE AGE

**"** When you feel in your gut what you are, and then dynamically pursue it – don't back down and don't give up – then you're going to mystify a lot of folks. **"** **BOB DYLAN**

**" Pop music tells you that everything is OK and rock music tells you that it's not, but that you can change it. "**
BONO, U2

**"** I met someone the other night who's 28 years old, and he hasn't worked a day since he left college because he's pursuing a dream he'll never, ever realise: he thinks he's a great singer. Actually, he's crap. But nobody has said to him, 'Why have you been wasting your time for eight years?' **"** **SIMON COWELL**

SIMON COWELL

**I didn't really have that slacker thing. Yeah, I'm a high school drop-out and I might have shown up late when I worked at Tower Records when I was 18. But playing in a band doesn't seem like work to me. It's my greatest passion. It's the one thing I can't do without.**

DAVE GROHL, NIRVANA

# "IT IS BETTER TO WIN THE PEACE AND TO LOSE THE WAR." BOB MARLEY

**We are all the same. No-one's on any higher level than anybody else. We've all got it within us for whatever we want to grasp for.** BOB DYLAN

While there's a certain selfish gratification in having any number of people buy your records and come to see you play, none of that holds a candle to simply hearing a song that I've written played by a band. Next to my wife and daughter, there's nothing that brings me more pleasure. **KURT COBAIN, NIRVANA**

**One of my favourite philosophical tenets is that people will only agree with you if they already agree with you. You do not change people's minds.** FRANK ZAPPA

Remember – the tedium is the message. **BRIAN ENO**

**I haven't really got a home anywhere. The earth's my home. I don't want to put down roots in case I get restless.** JIMI HENDRIX

Sometimes, it is a form of love just to talk to somebody that you have nothing in common with and still be fascinated by their presence. **DAVID BYRNE, TALKING HEADS**

**It's good to fail now and then – you learn a lot more out of failure than you do out of success.** IAN HUNTER

So, the thing is, if you really want to get it permanently, you have got to do it, you know... be healthy, don't eat meat, keep away from those night-clubs and meditate.
**GEORGE HARRISON**

**The act of creating is as integral a part of life as going to the lavatory.** DAVID BOWIE

The function of being an artist, for me, is that it is an experimental area where I can test out ways of thinking and operating and, hopefully, apply the result to real life. The advantages of testing them in an art contest is that it doesn't matter if you fail. **BRIAN ENO**

**I don't think Jimi (Hendrix) committed suicide in the conventional way. He just decided to exit when he wanted to.** ERIC BURDON, THE ANIMALS

Idiots that believe their own hypes, guys who start believing their own stuff, wind up in the most romantic place of all – six feet underground. **GENE SIMMONS, KISS**

**Whenever I see the news, it's about the same depressing things. Wars, hostages and people's arms hanging off with all the tendons hanging out, you know. So I tend not to watch it much. I prefer to go and see a movie or something where it's all done much more poetically. People getting their heads blown off in slow motion, very beautifully.** KATE BUSH

I have a New York code of ethics – speak unto others as you would have them speak unto you. In other words – watch your mouth! **LOU REED**

FRANK ZAPPA

**❝Death is a warm cloak. An old friend. I regard death as something that comes up on a roulette wheel every once in a while. ❞** GRAM PARSONS

**❝**Everyone in the world is getting fucked, one way or another. All you can do is see that you aren't fucking them directly. **❞**
**PAUL KANTNER, JEFFERSON AIRPLANE**

**❝It is sad that the air is the only thing we share. No matter how close we get to each other, there is always air between us. ❞** YOKO ONO

**❝**Most people wouldn't know good music if it came up and bit them in the arse. **❞ FRANK ZAPPA**

**❝It's an honourable thing to change your name. Women do it when they're married. ❞** BOB DYLAN, BORN ZIMMERMAN

**❝**So many people go through life without a direction. They just go from stop to stop. It's like they're on a bus and the only time they get off is to piss. **❞ TODD RUNDGREN**

**❝You have to keep busy. After all, no dog's ever pissed on a moving car. ❞** TOM WAITS

**❝**The thing is art always wins. Art will survive and I'm gong to die, so I'm not going to give art all the best moments of my life... the energy I have left after my art I save for love. **❞PATTI SMITH**

**❝Art is the perpetual motion of illusion. The highest purpose of art is to inspire. What else can you do? What else can you do for anyone but inspire them?❞** BOB DYLAN

**"** I'll just keep on rocking and hope for the best. **"**
**KEITH RICHARDS**

**" Groups are the working class of the leisure society. "**
ARTHUR BROWN

**"** The thought of being obscure doesn't bother me.
I've been obscure now for thirty-four and a half years.
It's not bound to bother me now. **"** IAN DURY

**" You can get money if you want it. You can get whatever
you want. It's called 'effort'. It doesn't take much – just a
lot of guts, in which the majority of the general public
seem to be lacking. "** JOHNNY ROTTEN

**"** Fuzzy hair is radiant. My hair is electric. It picks up all the
vibrations. **"** JIMI HENDRIX

**" Never underestimate people's ability to not know when
they're in pain. "** ART GARFUNKEL

**"** Without deviation, progress is not possible. **"** FRANK ZAPPA

**" The finest sensibilities of the age are convulsed with
pain. That means a change is at hand. "** LEONARD COHEN

**"** When you begin thinking you really are Number 1... that's
when you begin to go nowhere. **"** STEVIE WONDER

**" If you can see farther than today or tomorrow, if you can
see farther than that, then you're doing great. "**
VAN MORRISON

**"** We've always just gotten up there and played. We don't
have any dancers, we don't have all that stuff going on,
we just get up there and play. **"** LENNY KRAVITZ

**" Don't let your mouth write no cheque your tail
can't cash. "** BO DIDDLEY

"FROM 1989 TO WHEN I STOPPED TAKING DRUGS ON JUNE 5, 1998, I CAN HARDLY REMEMBER A THING." NOEL GALLAGHER, OASIS

# CHAPTER THIRTEEN
# TURN ON, DROP OUT

**"If you have children, you don't want to have drugs and drinks in the house. It's just not good."**
BILLIE JOE ARMSTRONG, GREEN DAY

**"**I like Amsterdam. But if I'm in the States or I'm in Mexico, I'm going to do my drugs regardless. It's cool that drugs are legal though. It's not cool that you can't smuggle shit out and take it home with you. What if you buy a bunch of weed and you can't smoke it all? You want to take it home with you, this shit you've paid for.**"** EMINEM

**"LSD is a medicine – a different kind of medicine. It makes you aware of the universe, so to speak. You realise how foolish objects are. But LSD is not for the groovy people, it's for mad, hateful people who want revenge. It's for people who have heart attacks. They ought to use it at the Geneva Convention."** BOB DYLAN

**"**When you smoke herb, you see the System so big in front of you, and the guys who control it no want that.**"**
BOB MARLEY

**"I heard that your brain stops growing when you start doing drugs. Let's see, I guess that makes me 19."**
STEVEN TYLER

**❝**I'm a tidy man. I keep my socks in the socks drawer and my stash in the stash box. Anything else they must have brought. **❞** GEORGE HARRISON, ON HIS BUST FOR MARIJUANA, 1969

**❝I'm glad they didn't have drugs in the Sixties when I was in high school, because if they'd had drugs, I'd still be in high school. ❞** JOE WALSH, EAGLES

**❝**I'd like people to be lifted up by the music, sure, but not to be thrown against the ground the next minute. A lot of music seems to be like that. It's like a drug. Maybe U2 music is a drug. I hope not. **❞** BONO

**❝The greatest thing I discovered at university was marijuana. ❞** HUGH CORNWELL, THE STRANGLERS

**❝REHAB IS A COP-OUT.❞** AMY WINEHOUSE

**❝We got spiked with Angel Dust once in Cleveland by two different lots of fucking hippies. That's an interesting drug. It makes you want to jump through car windscreens while they're going along. ❞**
LEMMY, MOTÖRHEAD

**❝**I was just a young chick. I just wanted to get it on. I wanted to smoke dope, take dope, lick dope, suck dope, fuck dope, anything I could lay my hands on I wanted to do it, man. **❞** JANIS JOPLIN

**❝I had to stop drinking. The thing was, I didn't know how to do it. I needed to be dowsed in cold water and told not to be silly, so that's what I did in rehab - I dowsed myself in cold water and told myself not to be silly! And I'm also quite spiritual, which helps me look after myself. I meditate every day, and I pray every morning and evening. ❞** ROBBIE WILLIAMS

**"**I can't understand why anybody should devote their lives to a cause like dope. It's the most boring pastime I can think of. It ranks a close second to TV.**"** FRANK ZAPPA

**"Pop music is just hard work, long hours, and a lot of drugs. "** MAMA CASS ELLIOT, THE MAMAS AND THE PAPAS

**"**We were definitely hot. That love, peace and granola shit went over real well.**"**
**DAVID CROSBY, HEARING C,S,N & Y'S 'WOODSTOCK' AGAIN IN 1977**

**"People have a mental picture of me because this whole business is run on rumours – Ozzy eats bats, Ozzy drinks urine. They read I'm crazy, a drug addict, alcoholic and don't give a fuck for anyone. That's true, but I don't take myself seriously. "** OZZY OSBOURNE

**"**Grass, it sits you down on your fanny – you can't do anything but see things.**"** JONI MITCHELL

**"I've never had a problem with drugs. I've had problems with the police. "** KEITH RICHARDS

**"**We were passing round a joint – a doobie – and someone said 'We're all doobie brothers'. We were called Pud before that.**"** THE DOOBIE BROTHERS

**"The whole hippie scene is wishful thinking. They wish they could love, but they're full of shit. "** FRANK ZAPPA

**"**Now everybody's seen God and so, big deal, it ain't even cool any more.**"** JERRY GARCIA, GRATEFUL DEAD

**"I tried marijuana one time, but it didn't give me anything but a headache. "** GLEN CAMPBELL

**"**Dad was cremated and I couldn't resist grinding him up with a little bit of blow...**"** KEITH RICHARDS

"CAN A WHITE MAN SING THE BLUES? I DON'T CARE A DAMN IF HE'S GREEN OR PURPLE – HE CAN GIVE IT TO YA." RAY CHARLES

# CHAPTER FOURTEEN
# GIFTED
# AND BLACK?

**❝I've read some amazingly derogatory things about me over the years and I've sat there and thought: if you replaced 'ginger' with 'black' or even 'Asian', you'd be up in front of a judge.❞** MICK HUCKNALL, SIMPLY RED

**❝**Whiskey, women and money are in all my songs and if you haven't experienced these, you haven't lived.**❞**
BROWNIE McGHEE

**❝The kind of blues I play, there's no money in it. You makes a good living when you gets established like I am, but you don't get that kind of overnight million-dollar thing, man... no way.❞** MUDDY WATERS

**❝**My son don't have to say it loud, I'm black and I'm proud. He don't have to be called those crazy names.**❞**
JAMES BROWN

**❝You get a lot of rappers saying, 'Yo, we got money now, everyone's eating, everything is good, you know what I'm saying?' Well obviously everything isn't good, and I don't know what you're saying, because a lot of rappers aren't saying nothing on records right now.❞** DMC, RUN DMC

> Rock'n'roll came from the slaves singing gospel in the fields. Their lives were hell and they used music to lift out of it, to take them away. That's what rock'n'roll should do – take you to a better place.
**MEAT LOAF**

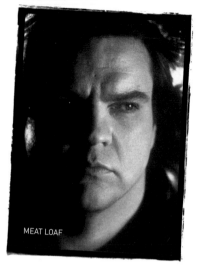
MEAT LOAF

> The whites just startin' to get the blues.
JOHN LEE HOOKER

> I was a soul boy before I was a punk. James Brown and Motown – we related to it because we were kind of blue collar. **MICK HUCKNALL, SIMPLY RED**

> The blues are almost sacred to some people, but others don't understand and when I can't make them understand, it makes me feel bad because they mean so much to me. BB KING

> When I sing the blues, when I'm singing the real blues, I'm singing what I feel. Some people maybe want to laugh, maybe I don't talk so good and they don't understand, you know? But when we sing the blues – when I sing the blues it come from the heart. From right here in your soul, an' if you singing what you really feel it come out all over. It ain't just what you saying, it pours out of you. Sweat runnin' down your face. **MUDDY WATERS**

**I'm still the flyest motherfucker out there. I'm still dictating what's hot, what the flavour is, what dance should be done. I'm not trying to hold on to my youth – I'm just timeless, I guess.**
PUFF DADDY/DIDDY/SEAN COMBS

# "ROCK'N'ROLL IS MUCH EASIER IF YOU'RE WHITE." KID ROCK

**I've said that playing the blues is like having to be black twice. Stevie Ray Vaughan missed on both counts, but I never noticed.** BB KING

Can't no white man sing the blues and can't no Negro sing no love song. **HOUND DOG TAYLOR**

**I was booed off stage in the early days – but I just didn't give a fuck. I started going round Detroit with MCs and winning rap competitions. I was like 'You may as will give me my respect, because I'll take it either way'. Nowadays, it's not about being black or white; if you've got the talent and somebody still tells you you can't rap, then fuck you and fuck them.** EMINEM

Our folks was in slavery a long time ago... it's all they could do on the field or farm is moan. That's the only way they could express their minds and get a little happy, to sing sad songs. **JOHN LEE HOOKER**

**You see I done get too old to get a job. Now I really got to stay with the music.** HOWLIN' WOLF (CHESTER BURNETT)

The blues is the truth. You'd better believe what they're telling you is the truth. **BUDDY GUY**

❝ To me, rappers are liars until I see that their actions coincide with what they said through the music. Me, I put my situations down and I make fun of them. ❞ 50 CENT

❝ I'm just doing what I do best and that's what makes good music, and that's how you can relate to people. ❞
**SNOOP DOGG**

❝ I rap in such a way where the hood can respect it but I can sit right in front of a white executive and spit the exact same verse and he'll understand at least 80% of it. ❞ KANYE WEST

❝ I don't think you can feel the blues until you been through some hard times. ❞ **MUDDY WATERS**

❝ **YOU KNOW... YOUNG PEOPLE THOUGHT THE BLUES WAS ENGLISH.** ❞ MEMPHIS SLIM

❝ I'm still deliverin', cos I've got a long memory. ❞
**MUDDY WATERS**

❝ Was it hard to win respect from the homies? Sure, I had to work hard to prove myself – a lot harder than the average rapper who's black. But that's only natural; rap is a predominantly black music. If I'm coming into this game, I've got to work harder if I don't want to get looked at as a joke. ❞ EMINEM

❝ For a fact, rock'n'roll ain't no different from the blues. We just pepped it up a lot... it's all trend, they come and go. It seems that like every twenty years the world jumps off and gets happy. It's going to explode again. You just be there when it jumps. ❞ **BIG JOE TURNER**

**❝I had to be darkened down so that the show could go on in dynamic-arsed Detroit. It's like they say, there's no damn business like show business. You had to smile to keep from throwing up. ❞** BILLIE HOLLIDAY

**❝**I don't know why it's happened. It's something I can't figure out myself. But as time marches by they understand the meaning of the blues...**❞ JOHN LEE HOOKER**

**❝All my life I was having trouble with women... I've done a lot of writing about women. Then, after I quit having trouble with them, I could feel in my heart that someone would always have trouble with them, so I kept writing those blues. ❞** MUDDY WATERS

**❝**I don't play anything but the blues, but now I could never make no money on nothin' but the blues. That's why I wasn't interested in nothin' else. **❞**
**HOWLIN' WOLF**
**(CHESTER BURNETT)**

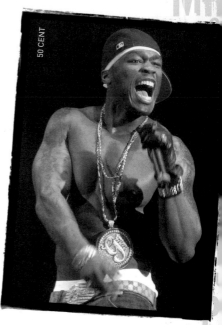

50 CENT

**❝Eminem is the rapper's rapper. He listens to everything. Every word, every slang, if you change something he's going to hear it all. ❞** 50 CENT

**"**All my life I've been dealing with my race because of where I grew up and being in the rap game. I'm at a boiling point. Anybody who pulls the race card is getting it right back in their face.**"**
**EMINEM**

**"Eminem is so talented it becomes annoying. Every time we go to the studio, he's got something new to play and it's like 'Oh man, I gotta have something new to play, too.'"** 50 CENT

**"**Soul ain't nothin' but a feelin'. It gets in your hand, makes you clap your hand. Get on your feet, makes you move your feet. That's all it is.**"** **WILSON PICKETT**

**"The kind of soul I'm talking about has got the grease. Ain't nothin' no good without the grease."** TINA TURNER

**"**You'll excuse me. I don't consider myself to be a black performer. I consider myself to be a performer who is black.**"** **STEVIE WONDER**

**Going to radio with a rap record prior to going to the consumer is like having no foreplay with your girlfriend.** LYOR COHEN, DEF JAM RECORDS

Rap fans are quick to forget what they appreciated just last year. **TRUGOY, DE LA SOUL**

**In my opinion, blues is a thing... you have the blues about something. Maybe you're broke, you're disgusted, you have bills you're losing your home, your car, your girlfriend – that's the blues... Blues come out of sadness, trouble, misfortune...** JOHN LEE HOOKER

When black people unite, the white man will unite and the Chinaman will unite, but black people must unite first. **BOB MARLEY**

## "HE DOESN'T SEEM LIKE THE SORT OF BLOKE WE WANT IN THIS COUNTRY."

AUSTRALIAN IMMIGRATION MINISTER KEVIN ANDREWS, ON WHY SNOOP DOGG WAS REFUSED ENTRY INTO AUSTRALIA.

That's where the blues start: it don't start in no city, now. Don't never get that wrong. It started right behind one of them mules or one of them log houses, one of them long camps or the levee camp. That's where the blues sprung from. I know what I'm talking about. **BUKKA WHITE**

"I'VE BEEN ASKED IF THIS IS THE LAST TOUR SINCE I WAS NINETEEN YEARS OLD."

MICK JAGGER

# CHAPTER FIFTEEN
# SIZZLING SOUNDBITES

**"Punk rock is a bad scene. I don't understand why it has to exist when there's so much in life."** FRANK SINATRA

**"**I haven't seen any of Warhol's films, but of course they stink of titillation.**"** CLIFF RICHARD

**"Believe it or not, I loved acid rock in college – and I still do."** CONDOLEEZA RICE, US SECRETARY OF STATE

**"***NSYNC have become Andy Warhol's tomato-soup can. And I can buy into why people dig it.**"**
**SHIRLEY MANSON, GARBAGE**

**"This group not only come out with obscenities in their programme, but they also bring the dope peddlers and the filth peddlers in their wake."**
COUNCILLOR RAY DAVIES OF CAERPHILLY, ON THE SEX PISTOLS

**"**Seeing someone fuck a monkey doesn't particularly shock me. I get much more shocked by someone attacking someone else for doing it.**"** **ROBERT SMITH, THE CURE**

**"AC/DC's Highway To Hell is the greatest meshing of vocal, guitar and content I've ever heard. That's what I aspire to."** BONNIE RAITT

**Ours is the folk music of the technological age.**
JIMMY PAGE, LED ZEPPELIN

**Journalists are a species of foul vermin, I mean I wouldn't hire people like you to guard my sewer. Journalists are morons, idiots, I don't perform to idiots. Journalists are ignorant and stupid.** LOU REED

# "THE ONE THING THAT CAN SOLVE MOST OF OUR PROBLEMS IS DANCING."
JAMES BROWN

**Rock'n'roll is the most brutal, ugly, vicious form of expression – sly, lewd, in plain fact, dirty... rancid smelling, aphrodisiac... the martial music of every delinquent on the face of the earth.** FRANK SINATRA

Slipknot are nothing to do with rock'n'roll. They're not a rock band, they've got no tunes, no chords or choruses. I came from The Beatles and Little Richard, they come from the circus. Maybe I'm too old to get it, but I don't mind because they're crap. **LEMMY, MOTÖRHEAD**

**We elected our man Nixon, President, and if you don't stand behind, him, get the hell out of the way so that I can stand behind him.** JOHNNY CASH

I got so many hits y'all can't handle me. I got more hits than Madonna's got kids. **PRINCE**

**I'm not as bad in the way they'd like to think I am. But I'm bad in a different way. I'm always going to be bad. More bad than Michael Jackson, but that's probably not a good comparison, considering.** MARILYN MANSON

> **If you want to take my picture, it'll cost you a fiver. If not, I'll smash your camera.**
> **SID VICIOUS, TO A PHOTOGRAPHER**

SID VICIOUS

> **It would be fucking monotonous if every show was good.**
> JOHNNY ROTTEN, SEX PISTOLS

> **I got my self-respect in this group. I don't believe in guitar heroes. If I walk to the front of the stage, it's because I want to reach the audience, I want to communicate with them. I don't want them to suck my guitar off.**
> **MICK JONES, THE CLASH**

> **I might not like it when a crowd shouts at me, but I certainly thrive on it..** DEBBIE HARRY, BLONDIE

> **Our fans in England are crazy. You can't stop them. They bite and claw their way on stage. We have to encourage the rest of the audience to beat them senseless.** **SID VICIOUS**

> **People were just asking for it. All those nude, fat people. They had victims' faces.**
> KEITH RICHARDS, ON THE MURDER AT ALTAMONT

> **Most rock journalism is people who can't write interviewing people who can't talk for people who can't read.** **FRANK ZAPPA**

> **Rock'n'roll is not meant to be criticised. If you can find someone who's willing to pay you to be a critic, then you've found a sucker.** PAUL STANLEY, KISS

**"**If you feel like singing along, don't.**"** JAMES TAYLOR

**"**You (one side of the audience) are Life. You (the other side) are Death. I straddle the fence and my balls hurt.**"** JIM MORRISON, THE DOORS

ELTON JOHN

**"**I find it a bit of a drag that certain people need to project their death wishes on me. I've no preoccupation with death whatsoever.**"** KEITH RICHARDS

**"**I got away with it because there were so many kids who could identify with me. Sure, they would all have loved to look like Keith Richards and live the life he leads, but I gave them some kind of hope.**"**

ELTON JOHN, ON HIS STARDOM

**"**People expect a lot more of us than they do everybody else.**"** MICK JAGGER

**"**I was standing at the bar the other day and a guy came up to me and said, 'Ray, I like your songs, I think you're a very underrated songwriter, a poet really.' So I hit him over the head with a bottle.**"** RAY DAVIES

**"**The performer is strictly a product of the public's imagination. We're just a reflection of what people want. It's the audience that are fags if anything.**"** DAVID BOWIE

**"**You can't take a fucking record like other people take a Bible.**"** KEITH RICHARDS

**"** I hate doing interviews; I like spontaneity. I like to feel I get a kick out of what I do and to discuss it exhaustively is very destructive. **"** BRYAN FERRY, ROXY MUSIC

# "YEAH, FUCK ME! I WISH YOU ALL COULD FUCK ME!"

BILLIE JOE ARMSTRONG, GREEN DAY

**"** I feel a bit silly. If somebody's looking at me with rapture all over their face, I want to throw a bucket of water over them. **"** IAN DURY

**"** People want art. They want showbiz. They want to see you rush off in your limousine. **"** FREDDIE MERCURY, QUEEN

**"** Audiences are very much like the kids in Tommy's Holiday Camp – they want something without working for it. **"** PETE TOWNSHEND, THE WHO

**"** There's this theory about the nature of tragedy, that Aristotle didn't mean catharsis for the audience, but a purgation of emotion for the actors themselves. The audience is just a witness to the event taking place on stage. **"** JIM MORRISON, THE DOORS

**"** I see the faces beaming up at me as I destroy my £500 guitar. Why should they, poor bastards, dig that? They enjoy the destruction because they despise phoney values. The heavy price on a piece of tin called a musical instrument. It is so far beyond their reach it might as well not exist. **"** PETE TOWNSHEND, THE WHO

**"** I know people talk about me as being a gone cat, wacko, and I guess, in the context of rock'n'roll, that's valid. **"**

DAVID BYRNE, TALKING HEADS

They say, 'Well, fucking Rod's gone off to Hollywood with a movie star'. The cunts! I come from the same background they do. In England, all rock'n'roll comes from the working class. That's your only way of getting out of the rabble. I come from nothing. Then, all of a sudden, I'm faced with a lot of glamorous women. What the fuck am I going to do? **ROD STEWART**

**If they don't get the words, they'll get the music, because that really where it's at.** BRIAN WILSON

All we are doing is telling people to question what they are doing and if it doesn't satisfy them, to do what they want. I hate preaching, it's just encouragement. **MICK JONES, THE CLASH**

**At my concerts, most of the chicks are looking for liberation: they think I'm going to show them how to do it.** JANIS JOPLIN

I'm after getting people off their arses, who feel they're isolated – the misfits. **RAY DAVIES, THE KINKS**

**People say the fans love you, and you've got to be loyal to them. But in a year, they're going to love someone else. Where will that leave me? Nowhere, no money, no fans, no nothing.** GARY NUMAN

An English audience is like a good fuck. You hold hands with it for a while, you kiss it, you pet it and then it pays you off. **GLENN FREY, THE EAGLES**

**It's nice to see an act whose audience can't relate to them.** LEONARD COHEN, ON DEVO

People on the street, them ignorant, mon! None of them know how to live. All right, I don't say 'Don't teach them

about Marco Polo, but teach 'em of Selassie, I, too, or Marcus Garvey or some a dem people.' Else people grow up on the street ignorant.' **"**
**BOB MARLEY**

**"The public hungers to see talented young people kill themselves. "**
PAUL SIMON

**"**I don't feel I have any responsibility, no. Whoever it is that listens to my songs owes me nothing... I've never written any song that begins with the words, 'I've gathered you here tonight'. **"** **BOB DYLAN**

BOB MARLEY

**"If all we've achieved is someone wanting my autograph, then we've gone wrong. "** JOE STRUMMER, THE CLASH

**"**Half these people turn up at concerts to see if I'm going to drop dead on stage and they're so disappointed that I'm still around and writing and capable of performing without falling down and stumbling around. But I haven't OD'd... These people, they wanted me to OD, but they never offered me the dope to do it with. **"** LOU REED

**"Either those cats cool it, or we won't play! "**
KEITH RICHARDS AT ALTAMONT

"WE WOULD RATHER BE RICH THAN FAMOUS. THAT IS, MORE RICH AND SLIGHTLY LESS FAMOUS." JOHN LENNON

# CHAPTER SIXTEEN
# IT'S ONLY MONEY

**"There are two kinds of artists left: those who endorse Pepsi and those who simply won't. "** ANNIE LENNOX

**"For the first time in history, the artist is realising financial success in his lifetime. "** JOE WALSH, THE EAGLES

**"Do you know how many of my songs I own? Not a single one. Out of 16 albums, not a single one. They won't belong to my children. I won't be able to pass them on to my grandchildren. They belong to someone else. Why? It's my music. "** PRINCE

**"One thing that depresses me is that there are so many successful people that are fucking miserable with it. It's so important to have fun with your success. "** ELTON JOHN

**"Money's not important. I never think I want to make millions and millions of dollars but I don't want to have to worry about it. The more money you have the more problems you have. I went from making no money to making comparatively a lot and all I've had is problems. Life was simpler when I had no money, when I just barely survived. "** MADONNA

**Somebody said to me, 'But The Beatles were anti-materialistic.' That's a huge myth. John and I literally used to sit down and say, 'Now, let's write a swimming pool.'** PAUL McCARTNEY

**If you don't go for as much money as you can possibly get, then I think you're stupid.** MICK JAGGER

**I never thought Alice Cooper was ever that hip. Alice was character and an attitude I created. Alice was always a commodity.** ALICE COOPER

**The advantages are that if you're the songwriter you earn the most money. If you're a band member then you earn a living, no more and no less.** NOEL GALLAGHER, OASIS

**My world is very small. Money can't really improve it any. Money can just keep it from being smothered.** BOB DYLAN

BOB DYLAN

**You know we were rehearsing, and we are running through 'Waiting For The Man'... you know, 'Twenty six dollars in my hand' ... and I said, 'Hey, wait a minute, twenty-six dollars???' I mean, you can't even get a blowjob for twenty-six dollars these days, let alone some smack.** LOU REED, 1977

**If a song lives for a couple of years, it's a pretty good thing.** PAUL SIMON

**I am happy to make money. I want to make more money, make more music, eat Big Macs and drink Budweisers.** KID ROCK

" Just point me at the piano and give me my money, and, in fifteen minutes, I'll have 'em shaking, shouting, shivering and shacking. " JERRY LEE LEWIS

**" I never thought I'd be a failure, maybe sell a record or two, you know. But I honestly never dreamed it would be this big... it's as weird as I thought it would be. Worth waiting for, too. I'm pleased it didn't happen to me when I was eighteen or nineteen. I'd have really freaked out then and spent it all. "** ROD STEWART

" What's money? A man is a success if he gets up in the morning and gets to bed at night and in between he does what he wants to. " **BOB DYLAN**

**" I think Alice Cooper Cosmetics would be real neat and classy. Just think – I could appear on TV in a bath, look into the camera and advertise Alice Cooper Turtle Oil. "**
ALICE COOPER

" It has nothing to do with me if there's a lot of bootlegs of The Cure; I've never objected to them, no-one's ever had their tape recorder confiscated at a Cure show, it doesn't bother me in the slightest. " **ROBERT SMITH, THE CURE**

**" It's crucial that I should be marketed in the right way. "**
DEBBIE HARRY, BLONDIE

" Our attitude to freak-outs is that we would not play at one again unless they paid us three times our normal fee. "
**PINK FLOYD**

**" I have no use for bodyguards, but I have very specific use for two highly trained certified public accountants. "**
ELVIS PRESLEY

**❝**About all I'll end up with is a white suit and a thousand dollars.**❞** MICK JAGGER ON THE STONES 1975 TOUR OF AMERICA, FOR WHICH HE ACTUALLY EARNED AROUND $450,000

**❝They're always saying I'm a capitalistic pig. I suppose I am. But... it's good for my drumming.❞** KEITH MOON

**❝**One of our aims is to stay amateurs – as soon as we become professional we'll be ruined.**❞** RAY DAVIES, THE KINKS, 1965

**❝Sometimes I have to remember that this isn't a record retail store I'm running. It's supposed to be some kind of art.❞** PAUL McCARTNEY

**❝**I'm against those who were born with golden spoons in their mouths... they want a kick up the backside. I've earned everything myself. I've worked hard for it and I'm going to enjoy it in the next five to ten years.**❞** ROD STEWART

**❝I'm not a rich man. I owe a lot of money. Money runs through your fingers and it's gone. Everyone thinks we're loaded, that we're driving around in Bentleys. Let them think it. Every time you see the words Stone Roses, it's Stone Roses £20 million, Stone Roses £40 million, but it's gone.❞** IAN BROWN, STONE ROSES

**❝**I have one basic drive on my side that they can't defeat – greed.**❞** FRANK ZAPPA

**❝They say, 'How's it goin'?' and I say 'Great.' And then they go (affects empathetic voice), 'Tch, you know what, man? I'd really hate to be in your position, man. I mean, your life must be really hard.' And I'm thinking, what? You sell two fuckin' records in Gloucester, and you're**

telling me you'd hate to be in my position? I've got a fuckin' Rolls-Royce and a fuckin' bastard mansion, and an airplane and you'd hate to be me? Ha, not as much as I'd fuckin' hate to be you... **"** NOEL GALLAGHER, OASIS

**"** Listen, if they're going to buy lunch-boxes, they may as well buy David Cassidy lunch-boxes. **"** **DAVID CASSIDY**

**"** I've no time for love affairs. You wake up in the morning – even when you've a day off – and the phone will ring: 'Can you come into the office?'... Your solicitor will phone you up, or your accountant, or manager or publicist. Then, you have everyday things to worry about. Like your car will go wrong, or your stove will blow up. It's amazing how many things will go wrong in life. **"** ELTON JOHN

**"NOBODY BELIEVES ME THAT I CAME INTO MUSIC JUST BECAUSE I WANTED THE BREAD. "** MICK JAGGER

**"** I'm happiest when I'm wasting myself, working. That's my reward, not money. I spend money like fucking water. I tried to eat a $100 bill the other day: couldn't get it down. **"** IAN DURY

**"** I probably made millions, but I ain't never seen none of it. **"** BO DIDDLEY

**"** I've got all the money I need. I could retire tomorrow if I wanted to. It's not about money any more. It's about egos; I wanna go out there and be the biggest band in the world and sell more records than anyone else. And I'm not gonna compromise that for anything. **"** LARS ULRICH, METALLICA

"It's been suggested that (Heather Mills) married me for the money and there is not an ounce of truth in this. She is a very generous person who spends most of her time trying to help others in greater need than herself. All the work she does is unpaid, so these stories are ridiculous and completely unfounded. I'm very sad to see that some insensitive people would choose a moment like this to spread these vicious rumours." **PAUL McCARTNEY**

"In this Jubilee year, I feel that it is only fitting that we should sign with a British company."

MICK JAGGER, ON SIGNING WITH EMI, 1977

## "HIT RECORDS ARE VERY NEAR AND DEAR TO ME." PETE TOWNSHEND, THE WHO

"Money means mostly a convenience for me. Cabs. I like getting out of a movie, if the movie is boring, in the middle and not feeling I've wasted the money I've spent." ART GARFUNKEL

"You can't have anarchy without a whole lot of money."
**PHIL LESH, GRATEFUL DEAD**

"You are not what you own." FUGAZI

"Yeah, being a multi-millionaire is a big, bad pain in the ass, man you wouldn't want to wish that on anybody."
**NOEL GALLAGHER, OASIS**

"The only difference between 'boring' and 'laid back' is one million dollars." GLENN FREY, THE EAGLES

**❝**I'm so tight, I don't spend a penny. I don't mind buying a round, but I can't stand buying two.**❞** ROD STEWART

**❝We had the same fights we had when we were poor, except 'that's my tomato you're eating' became 'that's my limousine, get your arse out'.❞** ALICE COOPER

ELVIS PRESLEY

**❝**Sharing money is what gives it its value.**❞** ELVIS PRESLEY

**❝Of course, we want to make more money and know where it goes. Why be naive about it? Why die like Stephen Foster, in the Bowery, slitting his wrists after writing all those wonderful standards?❞**

GLENN FREY, THE EAGLES

**❝**I was sixty-two the day they had the premiere of **A Hard Day's Night** and we all went to the Dorchester. Then Paul handed me a big parcel and I opened it and it was a picture of a horse. So I said 'Very nice' but I thought, 'What do I want with a picture of a horse?' Then Paul must have seen my face because he said 'It's not just a picture, Dad, I've bought you the bloody horse.'**❞** JAMES McCARTNEY

**❝It's easy to be independent when you've got money. But to be independent when you haven't got a thing — that's the Lord's test.❞** MAHALIA JACKSON

"APPARENTLY I'VE GOT LOADS
OF SELF-ESTEEM ISSUES...
I THOUGHT I WAS ALL RIGHT!"

PETE DOHERTY, BABYSHAMBLES

# CHAPTER SEVENTEEN
# ME AND MY EGO

> "I don't honestly feel I'm that important in musical history. That's not being humble, that's just fact."
> PAUL WELLER

> "The reason we're successful, darling? My overall charisma, of course." FREDDIE MERCURY, QUEEN

> "Growing up [as a] punk, 'rock star' was a derogatory term. As far as I'm concerned, it still is. Being a 'rock star' is about celebrity, not about music, which is why you're supposed to be doing this in the first place. Being a rock star shouldn't be considered a career option... If you don't love to play music – and you're not doing it purely for that reason – then quit."
> DAVE GROHL, FOO FIGHTERS

> "My bullshit is worth most people's diamonds." LOU REED

> "I wish I could work for someone like Paula Abdul. Honest to God, I am the kindest-of-kind human beings."
> PAULA ABDUL

> "U2 is an original species... there are colours and feelings and emotional terrain that we occupy that is ours and ours alone." BONO

❝You know, sometimes I look back on my life and wonder just how one man could achieve all I've done.❞
JAMES BROWN

❝We're not arrogant, we just believe we're the best band in the world.❞ NOEL GALLAGHER, OASIS

❝To suddenly become known by a lot of people because I waggled my arse at somebody isn't brilliant, is it? I'd rather be known for something better than that. Although my arse-wiggling is second to none, I'd rather people remembered me for what I create.❞
JARVIS COCKER

❝There is no critic in the world that knows as much as I do.❞ MILES DAVIES

MICHAEL JACKSON

❝I can spot empty flattery and know exactly where I stand. In the end it's really only my own approval or disapproval that means anything.❞
AGNETHA FALTSKOG, ABBA

❝I go around the world dealing with running and hiding... I can't take a walk in the park. I can't go to the store... I have to hide in the room. You feel like you're in prison.❞ MICHAEL JACKSON

❝I have an ego and I have to satisfy it. At the same time I have to live with my inglorious past [as a member of Led Zeppelin]. The thing I'm most proud of in the work I've been involved with has been the fact that I didn't care what happened to it as long as I cared for myself. It was very personal, very self-centred and very right, even if it wasn't palatable. " ROBERT PLANT, LED ZEPPELIN

" I wish my hair was thicker, and I wish my feet were prettier. My toes are really ugly. I wish my ears were smaller. And my nose could be smaller too. "
**BRITNEY SPEARS**

" I have a lick that's better than Jeff Beck's and Jeff has a lick that's better than mine, but Jimi Hendrix is better than either of us. " ERIC CLAPTON

" Who else is on the bill? "
**LEVON HELM, THE HAWKS, RESPONDING TO BOB DYLAN'S INVITATION TO JOIN HIM ON HIS 1966 TOUR**

" Normally, they want me to be rude to **them.** People come up to me and sing, and I say 'That was great. Thank you.' And they're like 'Well, aren't you going to be rude to me?' No! When I miss auditions, contestants get upset that I'm not there, because they expect me to be cruel to them - it's some sort of badge of honour. That's how crazy everything is. " SIMON COWELL

" Oh, sure. I dug the fame, the power, the money, and playing to big crowds. Conquering America was the best thing. " **JOHN LENNON**

" I didn't change my name in honour of Dylan Thomas, that's just a story. I've done more for Dylan Thomas than he's done for me. Look how many kids are probably reading his poetry now because they heard that. "
BOB DYLAN

" There's nobody in the world can make better records than I do. " **PHIL SPECTOR**

❝I started reading the papers about me being the 'Godfather of Punk' and I figured well, if I'm going to be the Godfather, then I'm going to be a real Godfather, Mafia-style. Taking no shit from no-one and screwing anyone who tried to screw me.❞ IGGY POP

❝I love being a star more than life itself.❞ JANIS JOPLIN

❝We're the only honest band that's hit this planet in about two million years.❞ JOHNNY ROTTEN

❝The last great concert I saw? Must've been our own show on YouTube. I was watching our Moscow show from 1991 and thinking, 'Damn, we were good that night. What happened?'❞ KIRK HAMMETT, METALLICA

❝Everyone's calling me eccentric. If that means I'm not average, then I guess I am.❞ PHIL SPECTOR

❝Hell, I'm only country.❞
**JERRY LEE LEWIS, RESPONDING TO THE PRESS OUTCRY AFTER HIS MARRIAGE TO HIS COUSIN MYRA, AGED 13**

# ❝IN MY IMAGINATION, I INVENTED PUNK ROCK A THOUSAND TIMES.❞

PETE TOWNSHEND, THE WHO

❝You have permission to call me anything except sir, all right? Lord of lords, your demigodness, that'll do.❞
**BONO, AFTER RECEIVING AN HONORARY BRITISH KNIGHTHOOD**

❝I'm not being big-headed, but The Kinks were unique... it's like getting to the North Pole first. Really, until we started diversifying, we couldn't be touched. We were a better group afterwards, but we became touchable.❞
RAY DAVIES, THE KINKS

**"** You must be vulnerable to be sensitive to reality. And to me, being vulnerable is just another way of saying that one has nothing more to lose. I don't have anything but darkness to lose. **"** **BOB DYLAN**

**" I'm told that I'm a parody of myself. But who better to parody? If I'm going to mimic somebody, I might as well mimic somebody good. Like myself. I can do Lou Reed better than most people and a lot of people try. "**
LOU REED

**"** I am today's powerful young man, I am today's successful young man. **"** **PETE TOWNSHEND, THE WHO**

**" As long as my picture is on the front page, I don't care what they say about me on page ninety-six. "** MICK JAGGER

**"** I am the biggest, the baddest and the fastest in the land. **"**
**BO DIDDLEY**

MADONNA

**" My children adore all that I do, they love dance music. My husband isn't a great fan. "**
MADONNA

**"** When I first realised I was good looking, I was naked, looking at myself in the mirror. Then, later, I got around to looking at my face. **"** **DAVID BOWIE**

**" I really believe that I have more talent in my little finger than Tony Bennett or anybody like that can possibly ever hope to achieve in a lifetime. "** ELTON JOHN

❝I wasn't born with a wig and make-up, and I could be very stylish if I chose to be. But I would never stoop so low as to be fashionable.❞ DOLLY PARTON

❝I don't care what Johnny Rotten says about me. Everything he says is only because he loves me 'cos I'm so good. He says nasty things about me because he has to. Because, along with the Queen, y'know, I'm one of the best things England's got. Me, and the Queen.❞

MICK JAGGER

MICK JAGGER

❝It's so fabulous being young and a girl and you can have nice clothes and can dress up and that's the nicest part about it, being famous and people admiring you.❞

SANDIE SHAW

❝I don't think people mind if I'm conceited. Every rock'n'roll star in the world is conceited.❞

MICK JAGGER

❝I'm more of a personality, a personality-cum-singer, than a singer-personality. There's twenty million people out there can sing me out of the fucking room, but they're not getting anywhere because they can only sing.❞

RINGO STARR

❝For a start, the band is much more handsome since I joined.❞

SID VICIOUS, ON REPLACING GLEN MATLOCK IN THE SEX PISTOLS

**"**I hope I don't go this week, because I'd only get a few lines on page three.**"**
**MARC BOLAN, ON ELVIS PRESLEY'S DEATH. HE HIMSELF DIED A MONTH LATER**

**"I've got fifty-six gold singles, and fourteen gold albums and if anyone out there doubts it, if you ever come through Memphis you can come argue about it, 'cos I've got every one of them hanging on the wall."** ELVIS PRESLEY

**"**I can be my gimmick, so at least I won't be overlooked. Whether I'm good or bad, you will see me coming. And you will know it when I walk in.**"**
**DOLLY PARTON, ON HER MASSIVE TRADEMARK BLONDE WIG**

**"Everything I know I taught myself."** BO DIDDLEY

**"**Sometimes I just like being Lou Reed better than I like being anyone else.**" LOU REED**

**"Me and Nureyev have flaming rows about whether it takes more talent and discipline to be a ballet dancer or a pop singer."** MICK JAGGER

**"**I never considered myself the greatest, but I am the best.**" JERRY LEE LEWIS**

**"I don't feel I could be a Michelangelo or a da Vinci. Those guys had too much isolation back then, they were given the nod. It's that for these days, so you're pretty much on your own. Michelangelo and da Vinci weren't on their own, they were pretty much supported."** BOB DYLAN

**"**I don't have the psychology of the fat girl. I don't hide in corners. I'm a very verbose person.**"**
**MAMA CASS ELLIOT, THE MAMAS AND THE PAPAS**

RITCHIE BLACKMORE

**❝I don't mind being thought of as a moody bastard. That's my thing. I wear black and don't give a fuck.❞**

RITCHIE BLACKMORE, DEEP PURPLE

**❝**I taught myself everything about piano. I was not influenced by anyone. I live so far back in the country, I don't think I knew anyone who could influence me. **❞**

JERRY LEE LEWIS

**❝The traditional rock star role is that you don't say anything. The best way to maintain your conceit is to keep your mouth shut and I'm certainly not prepared to do that. I couldn't. ❞** BRIAN ENO

**❝**I could have been a great songwriter. I reckon I could have been one of the greatest. I still write some. I just don't record any of them, because I prefer to concentrate on my entertaining instead. **❞** JERRY LEE LEWIS

**❝I believe that every band had their ten minutes of glory, but I like to think that we've left enough options open to give us twenty minutes. ❞** SUGGS, MADNESS

**❝**We make it so the worst we can possibly be is great. **❞**
GLENN FREY, THE EAGLES

**❝If you don't like my ideas, get the flyin' fuck out of here. I'll be damned if I'll have my music reduced to trivia and wimpo pussy rock. ❞** TED NUGENT

" I've got a car, a motorcycle, a truck, a house – what more could I possibly want? " **BRUCE SPRINGSTEEN, 1977**

" **I don't need people to tell me how good I am. I've worked it out for myself.** " ERIC CLAPTON

" I have a lot of respect for my own opinion. "
**PAUL STANLEY, KISS**

" **I'm just the same as ever – loud, electrifying and full of personal magnetism.** " LITTLE RICHARD

" I guarantee that if Elvis had his choice of being up in heaven right now, or coming on before me, he'd have to come on before me. There's no way Elvis can follow me. "
**JERRY LEE LEWIS**

" **I don't care who buys the records as long as they get to the black people so I will be remembered when I die.** "
MILES DAVIES

## "I'M JUST A LITTLE, INSIGNIFICANT BALD GUY. " MOBY

" **We always thought there was more to playing rock'n'roll than playing 'Johnny B. Goode'.** " PINK FLOYD

" I was the best wiggler in the world. " **MARC BOLAN**

" **When I was a boy, I was the hero in comic books and movies. I grew up believing in that dream. Now I've lived it out. That's all a man can ask for.** " ELVIS PRESLEY

"ONE NIGHT WITH [HER] MADE ME REALISE WHY KURT COBAIN KILLED HIMSELF."

LILY ALLEN, ON COURTNEY LOVE

# CHAPTER EIGHTEEN
# HOME TRUTHS

**"When Oasis and Blur were having their battle it felt like Radiohead were on the sidelines, holding everyone's coat. Then when we released OK Computer, it was like we gave them their coats back, all patched up... That battle they waged was depressing and belittling to both parties. Both groups were too naïve; they were functioning at a primary-school level of media manipulation."** COLIN GREENWOOD, RADIOHEAD

**"To sustain hatred is a very difficult thing to do, year after year. It's exhausting."** NICK CAVE

**"Courtney (Love) never even bothered to talk to say 'Hi' to me until I sold a million records. She's an opportunist and I wouldn't consider her a friend, barely an acquaintance, and the way she's behaved towards me in the media has seemed very exploitative in an unflattering way to her. So I'm not interested in being anything to her."** MARILYN MANSON

**"I've never bought a Dylan record. A singing poet? It just bores me to tears."** SIMON COWELL, ON BOB DYLAN.

**"People fail to realise that Bob Dylan was one of the greatest comedians ever."** ALICE COOPER

Every time I see the Spice Girls, it makes me want to try to fly by climbing my roof and strapping bricks to my shoes. **EDDIE VEDDER, PEARL JAM**

# "I HATE MADONNA! SHE LOOKS LIKE SHE STINKS!" ROBERT SMITH, THE CURE

Richard Ashcroft is a pompous dick from my experience. **WAYNE COYNE, FLAMING LIPS**

Brian Wilson is The Beach Boys. He is the band. We're his fucking messengers. He is all of it. Period. We're nothing. He's everything. DENNIS WILSON

A photograph of Keith Richards at his most wasted says more than anything just exactly what rock'n'roll is all about. **IAN HUNTER**

I remember the first time I saw the Stones. Our leader said, 'Don't watch them – they're a skiffle group.' RAY DAVIES, THE KINKS

When I see Damon Albarn, I buzz off him. If I was still caught up in it now I'd be a right wanker. **LIAM GALLAGHER, OASIS**

You know Damon, bless him, I've got a lot of respect for him. This never comes across in interviews, but I really do mean it. Because I'm indifferent to Damon, he thinks that I think he's a cunt. Our Liam will talk to him. I won't because he's just another singer in a band to me, but I don't think he's a cunt. Good luck to him. NOEL GALLAGHER, OASIS

**“** It's certainly not John Mayer and Avril Lavigne. Those people don't rock. If that's the young generation in the culture, then fuck it. **”** THURSTON MOORE, SONIC YOUTH

**“** Pop is short for popular, and to remain popular, you can't have a point of view or be outspoken. To remain popular you can't go against the grain. Janis Joplin, at this time, in this world, would not be a popular artist. Chrissie Hynde does not sell as many records as somebody like Mariah Carey. And that's because Mariah Carey and Whitney Houston don't have a fucking point of view. **”** MADONNA

**“** I'm not old enough to know a lot of them, but even I know Take That were bollocks. **”** ALEX TURNER, ARCTIC MONKEYS

**“** The only tribute I can give Marc is that he was the greatest little giant in the world. **”**
DAVID BOWIE MOURNS MARC BOLAN

**“I DON'T HAVE TO TRY TO BE A SEX BOMB, I AM ONE!”** KYLIE MINOGUE

**“** People think Paul Weller's some deep god, but he's a moany old bastard. He's like Victor Meldrew with a suntan. **”** NOEL GALLAGHER, OASIS

**“** I've been working so hard, I'm about to have a Mariah Carey. **”** USHER

**“** I wouldn't be surprised if (Madonna) made that African boy she adopted into a coat and wore him for 15 minutes, then threw it away. **”** MORRISSEY

" Buddy Holly always struck me as the type more likely to be found serving in a hamburger bar or delivering the soft drinks. " **PAUL ANKA**

**" Yeah, Wacko Jacko, where did that come from? Some English tabloid. I have a heart and I have feelings. I feel that when you do that to me. It's not nice. "**
MICHAEL JACKSON

" Paris Hilton... is a total raging, disgusting, rich, lazy party slut. Paris is fucking lame. I pray that my daughter will not turn out like her. " **DAVE GROHL, FOO FIGHTERS**

**" You know listening to Stink (sic) try to squeak through 'Roxanne' one more time, that's not fun. It's like letting air out of a balloon. "** JOHNNY ROTTEN ON STING

" Lauryn Hill is like to me the greatest artist in the last 25 or 30 years, but – still – if you mentally ill, you mentally ill. I'm not no expert, but based on my professional opinion, she needs medication. " **PRAS, FORMERLY OF THE FUGEES**

**" I'd join a band with John Lennon any day, but I wouldn't join a band with Paul McCartney. "** GEORGE HARRISON

" Actually, I never liked Dylan's music before I played with him. I always used to think he sounded like Yogi Bear. "
MICK RONSON

**" Put it like this. Let's raise the stakes. If Kanye West sells more records than 50 Cent on September 11, I'll no longer write music. I'll write music and work with my other artists, but I won't put out any more solo albums. "** 50 CENT

**❝**I can imagine him becoming a successful hairdresser. A singing Vidal Sassoon. **❞**

**MALCOLM McLAREN, MANAGER, SEX PISTOLS, ON JOHNNY ROTTEN, AFTER THE SEX PISTOLS SPLIT**

OZZY OSBOURNE

**❝What can you say about Pete Doherty? If you have to take heroin to be famous – well, I don't get it. Will Pete be a Kurt Cobain, Nirvana or a Jimi Hendrix? Never in a million years. He hasn't the talent to tune their guitars. ❞**

PETE WATERMAN, PRODUCER

**❝**I'd like to stop the 'industry' part of the music industry because right now there is a manufactured line of marketable pop boy and girl bands – 'nice-tits-puckered lips-keep the money rolling in'. It's a fucking assembly line! **❞ OZZY OSBOURNE**

**❝The Rolling Stones aren't rock. They're cabaret music. ❞**

MALCOLM McLAREN, MANAGER, SEX PISTOLS

**❝**There's no Robin Hoods in rock. That punk shit was just a little too trendy. Costello's OK, we played with him, but I couldn't call him Elvis. **❞ TOM PETTY**

**❝The Press try to categorise me as a 'gloom-and-doom' singer. But, take a look at Morrissey! That man's a professional moaner! ❞** ROBERT SMITH, THE CURE

**❝**I don't like people like Rod Stewart and Elton John and I don't like the way they carry on. I get very upset at being identified with that kind of person. I also don't talk to anyone who's a better singer than I am. **❞ MICK JAGGER**

**Thank God for The Beatles, they showed us a trick or two.** JERRY LEE LEWIS

# "YES AND GENESIS ARE AS EXCITING AS A USED KLEENEX." NICK LOWE

**The Rolling Stones are The Shadows plus 2000 decibels. And I never did think much of The Shadows.** TOMMY STEELE

You can't drink on an eight-hour flight, pass out, and then go on stage... well you can, but then you're Spandau Ballet. **ROBERT SMITH, THE CURE**

**It's time for Eminem to go. He's a fucking sexist. He's not good for my fucking daughter. I want a good world for my daughter. When I saw 'It's so boring without me' in that song ('Without Me'), I just figured he'd written a nice song about me!** COURTNEY LOVE

I was made to feel like I was a fat kid by Michael. He called me 'Fat Butt'. It really affected me, even as an adult. **JANET JACKSON**

**I have no respect for Jim Morrison, The Doors, I didn't even feel sorry for him when he died.** LOU REED

Whether or not he decides to join forces with the human race, Dylan's a genius. **JOAN BAEZ, 1969**

**I'm really sick of Beyonce.** RUFUS WAINWRIGHT

Take That had been micro-managed for years, and Robbie (Williams) suffered from being the youngest. He wasn't a team player, I wasn't either – I wanted to be team leader,

and so did he. I think he found it annoying playing second fiddle to anyone, it's not in his nature.' **"**
**GARY BARLOW, TAKE THAT**

**"As a person, I can't sing Dylan's nasty hateful songs. I can appreciate the honesty of them, and melodically they're good, but I can't sing them. "** JOAN BAEZ, 1969

**"**She was like a mum to us. **"**
**JOHN LENNON ON MEETING QUEEN ELIZABETH II**

**"I don't know John Lennon. The last thing he said to me was 'Fuck off'. "** RAY DAVIES, THE KINKS

**"**If you want to hear pretentiousness, just listen to John Lennon's 'Imagine'. All that 'possessions' crap. **"** LOU REED

**"Elvis was as big as the whole country itself, as big as the whole dream. Nothing will ever take the place of that guy. "** BRUCE SPRINGSTEEN

**"**I thought his name was about the weirdest that I ever heard. I thought for sure he was a black guy. **"**
**PAUL SIMON, ON ELVIS PRESLEY**

**"I'd rather spend my time looking at the sky than listening to Whitney Houston. "** ROBERT SMITH, THE CURE

**"**As usual there's a great woman behind every idiot. **"**
**JOHN LENNON ON YOKO ONO**

**Limp Bizkit? I could make a nice bracelet out of them, or a nice pair of earrings. They're just fucking pap, garbage. Sorry. We did the Ozzfest a couple of years ago, and I went out and had a look at them the first night, and they had a giant toilet on stage, into which they were throwing pictures of the Spice Girls. I thought, 'Wow, this is really cutting-edge shit!' "** LEMMY, MOTÖRHEAD

"Woody Guthrie, frankly was a genius writer, but Guthrie couldn't hold Seeger's socks as a human being."
**HARRY CHAPIN**

"Why should I be bored for another two hours after being bored for three years?"
RICK WAKEMAN, REFUSING TO ATTEND A YES GIG

"Dylan was what I'd always meant by the poet – someone about whom the word was never used." **LEONARD COHEN**

"I started off writing instrumentals. My idol at the time was Hank B Marvin, Cliff Richard's guitar player."
NEIL YOUNG

"I want to become a good actor, because you can't build a whole career on just singing. Look at Frank Sinatra. Until he added acting to singing he found himself slipping down hill." **ELVIS PRESLEY**

"Don't talk to me about Nirvana. He was a sad man who couldn't handle the fame. We're stronger than that. And you can fuck your fucking Pearl Jam."
LIAM GALLAGHER, OASIS

"That cunt is a great entertainer."
**PROMOTER BILL GRAHAM ON MICK JAGGER**

"Alice Cooper is the worst, most disgusting side of rock music." LOU REED

"I thought of Brian as a perfect gentleman, apart from buttering his head and trying to put it between two slices of bread." **TOM PETTY MEETS BRIAN WILSON**

"Mick Jagger is more of a showman than I am. And I'm more of a singer than he is. That's not a put-down of either of us." ROD STEWART

" Frank Zappa is probably the single most untalented person I've heard in my life. He's a two-bit, pretentious, academic and he can't play his way out of anything. He can't play rock'n'roll because he's a loser. And that's why he dresses so funny. He's not happy with himself and I think he's right. " **LOU REED**

" **You know, people like the Jefferson Airplane, Grateful Dead, all those people are just the most untalented bores that ever come up... I mean, can you take Grace Slick seriously? It's a joke, a joke. The kids are being hyped.** " LOU REED

" My greatest influences are The Beatles and Tchaikovsky. " **ROY WOOD**

" **Mick Jagger is the perfect pop star. There's nobody more perfect than Jagger. He's rude, he's ugly-attractive, he's brilliant. The Rolling Stones are the perfect pop group – they don't give a shit.** " ELTON JOHN

ELTON JOHN

" He was a cunt. He was great but he was a cunt and that's why I love him. " **ERIC BURDON ON JIMI HENDRIX**

" **I like Dylan's whole attitude. The way he dresses, the way he doesn't give a damn, the way he sings discords and plays discords. The way he sends up everything.** "
GEORGE HARRISON

" He stole my music but he gave me my name. "
**MUDDY WATERS ON MICK JAGGER**

**We've got absolutely no intention of ending up like The Tremeloes.** KEITH MOON

I think for the life spans he's lasted, Chuck Berry's productivity has been nil, more or less. ELTON JOHN

**Even my mom is calling me Shaggy now, which is weird, because Shaggy is more like a character that I play.**
SHAGGY

I would love for the time to come where somebody can talk about me and not have to talk about Britney and Christina in the same sentence. We're really, really different. JESSICA SIMPSON

**Mick Jagger loves to humiliate people, but he was nice to me because he needed the music.** RY COODER

Johnny Rotten is a paranoid clown.
**HUGH CORNWELL, THE STRANGLERS**

**Dylan gets on my nerves. If you were at a party with him, I think you'd tell him to shut up.** LOU REED

For a guy who is probably one of the funniest people you will ever meet, Liam actually has no sense of humour. He's never told a funny joke in his life.
**NOEL GALLAGHER, OASIS**

**Having played with other musicians, I don't even think The Beatles were that good.** GEORGE HARRISON